Straight Talk About Suffering

LAWRENCE W. WILSON

Beacon Hill Press of Kansas City
Kansas City, Missouri

Copyright 2005
by Lawrence W. Wilson and Beacon Hill Press of Kansas City

ISBN 083-412-2014

Printed in the
United States of America

Cover Design: Ted Ferguson

Library of Congress Cataloging-in-Publication Data

Wilson, Lawrence W., 1959-
    Why me? : straight talk about suffering / Lawrence W. Wilson.
        p. cm.
    Includes bibliographical references.
    ISBN 0-8341-2201-4 (pbk.)
    1. Suffering—Religious aspects—Christianity. 2. Suffering—Biblical teaching.
3. Consolation. I. Title.

    BV4909 .W57 2005
    248.8'6—dc22

                                                                2004026906

10 9 8 7 6 5 4 3 2 1

For Laurinda

CONTENTS

INTRODUCTION

*How can you lecture me about God when you
have no idea what I've suffered?*

Just as the sufferings of Christ flow over into our
lives, so also through Christ our comfort overflows.
—2 Cor. 1:5

I'm sure they meant well, but the words just didn't make sense to me. I nodded benignly and tried to look happy. I'm not sure if it was the Vicodin or the Holy Spirit who kept me smiling.

I was recovering from joint replacement surgery, about six weeks post-op. I had a new knee, along with a nine-inch scar, a cane, three rehab appointments a week, and a throbbing pain in my leg that just wouldn't go away. And I had one more thing—an appointment for bilateral hip replacement to be carried out within the next few weeks. It would be my second major surgery within four months, two trips to hell and back. And many people—friends of mine, family members, good people—tried to encourage me with words.

"Well, at least it'll all be over soon."

"I'll bet you'll be glad to get that second surgery done with."

"Look on the bright side—you're getting it all done at once!"

"In a few weeks, your life will be right back to normal."

I didn't bother to explain. Sure, joint replacement surgery is a helpful thing. My ability to walk depends upon it. In that sense, I was glad for it. But the surgery is painful. You lose part of your body. You suffer intense pain and endure weeks of paralyzing fatigue. And when it's over, you have to drop your pants to get through airport security. Who could want that? How could anyone think of it as normal?

Pain changes reality for those who suffer it. Life afterward just isn't the same as it was before. Most of the Vietnam veterans I've known did not return from their tour of duty and "get back to normal." Their old lives did not exist anymore. They learned to live with a new reality. Widows and widowers I've known did not "get on with life" after the death of a partner. Their lives had changed. Living and dying held new meaning for these who had looked death in the face. And I knew from experience that my own life would not return to normal after surgery. I would have less pain but would also have a prosthetic joint. Life would be better in some ways but worse in others. It would not be the same again.

But how could I tell my friends that? How could I make them understand that surgery may be helpful but that it's never good? How could I make them see reality? I decided not to try.

"Yeah, should be a blast. Can't wait. Now I think it's time for my pill."

IN SEARCH OF REALITY

Suffering is the central fact of our lives, yet most of us ignore it for as long as possible. We scrupulously avoid thinking about suffering, especially its ultimate form—death. We busy ourselves with work, we raise our children, we take vacations to the beach or to the mountains or to Disney World, telling ourselves that these weeklong reprieves from toil are what "real life" is supposed to be.

We know better.

People die, some of them young and not so distant from us. Children are born, not always healthy. Our own bodies show signs of wear, and the pains that used to evaporate with a good night's sleep linger for days. Some never leave. Sooner or later, it dawns on us that the world is not an entirely good place, and that realization causes us to wonder whether the God who created it is entirely good himself. We ask troubling questions: Why did this happen to me? Doesn't God care about my pain? What kind of God would allow people to suffer?

In questioning God about the problem of pain, we at least have come to the right place. It's right to lay the issue of suffering at God's doorstep, for if we trace any question about the world or ourselves back to its source, we'll find God. He is responsible for both. He is responsible for everything. Therefore, all our questions about suffering are really questions about him.

And we are free to ask them. No inquiry ever threatened either God's holiness or our salvation. God is pleased when we seek to learn, to grow, to explore our world, and to gain understanding. "For the LORD gives wisdom, and from his mouth come knowledge and understanding" (Prov. 2:6).

But here's a warning. Anyone who asks hard questions must be prepared for hard answers. Those who search for God don't always like what they find, for God is not made according to our image of him; he is not made at all. Rather, as he himself told Moses, God simply is what he is (see Exod. 3:14). We can love him or we can hate him, but we can't change him. We must deal with God—and with life—as they are, not as we wish them to be. We must be real.

That's why, when dealing with the problem of suffering, it's impossible to do either of two things: defend God or redeem pain.

Defending God

"Petitions seek to defend God," the headline declared. And so they did. On February 28, 2003, the Ninth United States Circuit Court of Appeals reaffirmed an earlier ruling that had declared the words "under God" in the United States' Pledge of Allegiance to the flag unconstitutional for use in public schools. Within five days more than 200,000 people swamped an online petition decrying the ruling. The petition gained 75,000 electronic signatures in the 48 hours following the court decision.[1] *God's having a bad day*, the signers must have figured. *Let's give him a hand and straighten this thing out.*

Lots of people want to defend God, as if he were helpless to defend himself. In fact, there's an entire branch of Christian theology devoted to the subject, apologetics, which is saddled with the impossible chore of making ideas like the resurrection of the dead seem rational. Entire careers have been devoted to trying to convince people first that God exists and second that he's really an OK guy. *If people only understood the facts*, we think, *if they would just listen to the whole story, then they would see the reason behind the things God does or doesn't do. They would understand the need for pain and suffering, and it wouldn't hurt so much. If we could just explain some things, God wouldn't look so bad.*

But a god in need of a lawyer is no god at all. If God is real, then he must be capable of speaking for himself whenever he chooses; usually he doesn't. God has already said most of what he has to say in the Bible, and he seldom elaborates on it. That's not to say that Scripture is an apology, meaning a defense, for God. It simply tells us who he is. We can take it or leave it.

Even when God does, rarely, choose to make special revelation, he seldom does so in response to critics. Like Jesus standing before Herod, God refuses to answer those who mock or threaten him.[2] And many of our questions about suffering, and therefore about God, are really accusations. Often the question "Why?" might be rendered "How dare you?" And that's a question God simply will not answer. So why should anyone else?

More to the point, defending God is of no value because it doesn't convince cynics, and it doesn't help seekers. The search for truth is a search for faith, not reason. And words have little value in communicating faith; arguments have none at all. The existence of God cannot be proven, as if he were a mathematical theory, and his actions cannot be explained, as if he were a machine. God must be believed, and the decision to believe is an individual choice that stands apart from reason. We believe in God not because it's logical to do so; we believe in him because he is real. And we do not trust God only when we finally understand him, but quite the reverse. We must trust him most precisely when we don't understand who he is or what he has done.

To be sure, friends can help on the journey to belief, and our intellect helps us to know God. But logic is not, finally, our connection with him; faith is. We trust God in spite of what we suffer.

And that can never be made easy.

Redeeming Pain

Strike One was when she sat on the bed. Besides being a common courtesy not to invade the personal space of a hospitalized person, it's the first thing they teach students in any counseling course. Apparently, the eager visitor who comforted my mother-in-law had never taken one. Strike Two was when she denied Diana's pain by glossing over it. For five minutes the visitor gushed clichéd statements like "That wasn't so bad, was it?" and "Isn't it wonderful what doctors can do these days?" and "You'll be back on your feet in no time." Finally, she opened the Bible and pulled out a magic wand that promised to turn something evil into something good. "Remember," the visitor lectured, "God does everything for a reason, so he must have a reason for putting you through this. I can't wait to see what God is doing in your life."

Strike Three. I couldn't put the visitor out, so I left the room appalled at the notion that cancer might be a "good thing" that "God did" to my mother-in-law.

Disease is not good, and not even God thinks it is. It's im-

possible to redeem suffering by pretending that pain is delightful. Pain hurts. Nobody wants it. That's why our questions
about suffering so often take an accusatory tone. The mere
presence of pain raises a question about the goodness of God.
It's true that we can learn from pain and through painful experiences and that we can benefit from them. But that does not
make pain itself anything other than excruciating.

Listen.

In 1942 Nazi "physicians" at the Dachau concentration
camp conducted a series of experiments on prisoners to study
the effects of hypothermia. In one set of experiments, prisoners were forced to endure a tank of ice water, sometimes for as
long as three hours. The victims rapidly developed extreme
rigor, and not surprisingly, many of them died. Some who survived were subjected to various rewarming techniques. Some
other prisoners screamed in pain as they were forced to remain naked in the open for several hours with temperatures
below freezing.[3]

Hideous as these experiments were, they did have a goal.
The Nazis wanted to gain information that would help the
Luftwaffe treat downed pilots, many of whom crashed into the
ice-cold North Atlantic. Presumably, the Nazis did learn something and perhaps even saved some lives as a result.

Would that make torture something good?

Pain and suffering are part of the curse that God placed on
the world, and there's nothing good about being cursed.[4] To be
sure, *we* are improved through suffering (see James 1:2–3). We
can learn through pain, and our faith can be perfected by it (see
Gen. 3:14–19). But suffering and death in themselves are not
good. Someday God will destroy them both (see Rev. 21:4;
22:3). We can accept suffering, we can endure pain, we can even
triumph over them, but nobody, not even God, asks us to like it.

So what's the point? If we can't escape suffering, if pain is a
constant companion, then how is it ever possible to enjoy life?

THE GOOD LIFE

Nathaniel Hawthorne, considered by many as America's first Christian literary giant, wrote a short story about a young man in Puritan New England who became obsessed with the existence of evil. Young Goodman Brown kissed his bride, Faith, good-bye one evening and began a journey through the forest. On his way, he met a collection of townsfolk who seemed to be headed in the same direction. There was Goody Cloyse, an old Sunday School teacher, and Deacon Gookin, a preacher. These good people were headed for a secret witches' meeting deep in the woods, where they would that night induct two new members into their evil circle.

Young Goodman Brown was shocked and terrified. Was it true that evil lurked in the heart of his own community? Could these good church folk really be witches? Goodman Brown secretly followed them until he came to the clearing where the coven had assembled. There he was appalled to see what appeared to be the whole collection of his friends and neighbors. Everyone was there, saint and sinner alike. Before he knew it, Goodman Brown himself was standing before the evil altar, side by side with another devotee ready to be inducted into the cult of wickedness. Just then, he looked toward the one standing near him. It was his own Faith! Screaming with fright, Goodman Brown fled that place, running back toward town.

The next morning the young man wandered into the village, exhausted and bewildered by what he had seen. Yet as he met the townspeople, none of them seemed to remember what had happened. The minister walked calmly along the street, meditating on his sermon. Goody Cloyse sat in her kitchen, teaching scripture to a child. Just hours before, these good people had joined hands with the devil. Was it all a dream?

Young Goodman Brown couldn't decide; but neither could he forget what he had seen. He brooded on it the rest of his life. There was evil in the world, in all its people, in his neighbors, in his own wife, even in himself.

> Often, awaking suddenly at midnight, he shrank from the bosom of Faith; and at morning or eventide, when the family knelt down at prayer, he scowled and muttered to himself, and gazed sternly at his wife, and turned away. And when he had lived long, and was borne to his grave . . . they carved no hopeful verse upon his tombstone, for his dying hour was gloom.[5]

The realization of Young Goodman Brown comes to each of us before we die. The reality of suffering causes us to ask hard questions about the world, about ourselves, and about God. The questions themselves frighten some into retreat. They shrink away from faith and away from God, living whatever remains of their lives in bitterness and anger. Like Goodman Brown, they die in gloom.

But another life is possible, and another death.

Many years ago I was a chaplain for the volunteer fire department in the tiny town where we lived. I had only two duties. One was to give either the invocation or the benediction at the fire company's annual dinner (the Catholic priest in town did the same). The other was to attend the wake for any Protestant fireman or his family member and lead the company in prayer. These firefighters were not overly pious souls, but they attended every wake in dress uniform and listened respectfully during the reading of scripture, then bowed their heads solemnly and recited the Lord's Prayer. It was an aging community; I attended a lot of wakes.

It was while we lived there that my first daughter was born, lived for five pain-filled months, and died. At her wake, while my wife and I sat helplessly beside the tiny wooden casket, a company of firefighters, wearing full-dress uniform, marched silently into the room. One of their number had been appointed to fill my place. He offered a brief prayer. Then the firefighters, many of them choking back tears, stepped quietly up to the front and shook my hand and hugged my wife. A few of them said something like "I'm real sorry," but most were unable to speak at all. They didn't have to. Their presence with us was comfort enough.

I will not say that their gesture made the death of my daughter easy to bear. What could possibly do that? Yet those firefighters seemed to know what preachers, teachers of religion, and the authors of books seem to forget: we have each other, and that's what we need most. To show compassion for those who suffer is far more important than to understand their experience or answer their questions. For in the end, there's no answer for a child's coffin.

It's not possible to defend God; he speaks for himself when necessary. Neither is it possible to find easy answers to life's most difficult questions; such answers do not exist. Yet we can find good and God in every circumstance, experience joy alongside pain, and live a good life and die a good death in spite of that nagging question "Why?"

That, I believe, is possible for every person. It is possible for you.

QUESTIONS FOR REFLECTION

1. Does thinking about death frighten you? Why or why not?

2. Have you ever wanted to ask God something about your experience of suffering or that of someone else? What would you ask him?

3. What is the best answer you've heard to a question about suffering? What is the worst?

4. Do you think people who are suffering can be happy? Why or why not?

εμαθεν αφ ων επαθεν
—ΠΡΟΣ ΕΒΡΑΙΟΥΣ

HE LEARNED OBEDIENCE
FROM WHAT HE SUFFERED.
— HEB. 5:8

1
THE PROBLEM OF PLEASURE
AND THE VALUE OF PAIN

How could a good God allow suffering?

From suffering, knowledge.
—Aeschylus, *Agamemnon*

California's San Fernando Valley is best known as the home of a half-dozen moderately fashionable suburbs of Los Angeles, including Studio City, North Hollywood, and Sherman Oaks. Americans got their first peek at the valley when Rowan and Martin broadcast their notorious *Laugh In* from "beautiful downtown Burbank." Viewers of daytime favorites like *The Price Is Right* still visit the valley every day. On the whole, it's a quiet place, unique only in that it has more than its share of celebrities—and those who want to be.

That makes the San Fernando Valley the ideal setting for another side of the entertainment business, pornography. Hidden among the valley's middle class homes and storefronts is a beehive of pornographic entrepreneurism: dozens of production companies employing some 1,200 "actors" and "actresses" churn out some $13 billion worth of sex videos each year. Not New York, not New Orleans, not even Las Vegas, but the suburbs northwest of Los Angeles are the "pleasure capital" of North America.

But on April 15, 2004, the business of pleasure ground to a halt. On that bright spring day, the cameras stopped rolling, the klieg lights went dark, and everybody put on their clothes and went home. Most adult filmmakers abruptly stopped production.

The shutdown was prompted by a crisis. The pornographers were scared straight after two of their stars were found to be carrying the AIDS virus. Forty-five performers were banned from working in the industry—those who tested positive and others who had had contact with them—and most adult production companies agreed to halt production for at least 60 days.

Interestingly, some performers were surprised by the discovery of the deadly virus in their midst.

"I'm really upset," said one 18-year-old who used the name "Randi Wright." "I'm angry at the person who brought it into the industry." Ms. Wright had begun working in adult films about a month prior to the shutdown to earn money for college tuition.[1] Like Captain Renault in the classic film *Casablanca*, she was "Shocked! Shocked!" to encounter a sexually transmitted disease in the sex trade.

It seems impossible that anyone who earns a living making pornography could be naive about the dangers associated with having multiple sex partners. Could Ms. Wright really have believed that no evil could come from indiscriminate sex?

Yet this young woman, at once worldly-wise and hopelessly naive, voices the view of pleasure held by most people. We think of it as an unqualified good, and we're always surprised to discover that it's not. What feels good, we reason, must be good. And certainly a good God would want what's good for us.

But there's a problem with that notion, the dirty little secret behind pleasure: it can kill you.

THE PROBLEM OF PLEASURE

Most of us equate pleasure with moral good. We firmly believe that life should be pleasant and comfortable and that human beings have a right—a divine right—to experience what we think of as the good life.

That belief did not spring from thin air. It was carefully planted in our psyche in the Garden of Eden, where Satan tempted Eve to do wrong by appealing to her sense of right. When you eat the forbidden fruit, Satan told her, "you will not surely die. . . . For God knows that when you eat of it your eyes will be opened, and you will be like God, knowing good and evil" (Gen. 3:4–5). The lie worked like a charm. For "when the woman saw that the fruit of the tree was *good* for food and *pleasing* to the eye, and also *desirable* for gaining wisdom, she took some and ate it" (Gen. 3:6, emphasis added).

What looks good must be good, Eve reasoned. If eating the fruit will make my life better, then it must be the right thing to do. Doesn't God want me to be happy?

Today the notion that pleasure is a moral good—indeed, a constitutional right—is cultivated by a consumer culture that hawks every ware from luxury cars to day-planning books with the maxim "It's all about you."[2]

Way back in the 1970s, McDonald's sold an eager public on the notion that "You deserve a break today." Believing that no one should be burdened with the drudgery of meal preparation, North Americans now spend $110 billion a year on fast food.

L'Oreal, a maker of hair care products, picked up the drumbeat with the slogan "It costs a little more, but I'm worth it." We now spend $8 billion a year on cosmetics.

In the 1980s, Disney cleverly used champion athletes to convince children that nothing on earth could rival a trip to its theme park. When asked seconds after winning the Super

Bowl what they planned to do, triumphant quarterbacks would grin into a camera and holler, "I'm going to Disney World!" A generation of families went with them; we now spend $9.6 billion a year on amusement parks.

And we spend another $8 billion on video games, $13 billion on chocolate, and $1 billion on tanning. The average new car costs $26,150 and has something like 100 electric motors that power everything from windshield wipers to seat backs, presumably because we believe that even the most mundane chores should be effortless. Like naive 18-year-olds, we're convinced that life should always be easy, enjoyable, diverting, and fun. Certainly that's what God wants. If he really is good, then he must want us to feel good all the time.

But here's the tragic secret: pleasure can hurt you, just like pain. It killed Adam and Eve, and it's been killing us ever since.

Many people shop in order to feel good. But the average household has more than $4,000 in credit card debt, and according to the American Bankruptcy Institute, personal bankruptcy filings have reached an all-time high, with 1.6 million consumers hitting bottom in 2002.[3] What's good about that?

Everybody takes pleasure in eating. Yet we face dozens of serious health problems caused by eating too much. Arkansas legislators are so concerned about the problem that they recently passed a state law aimed at reducing obesity in children.[4]

Pain-relieving drugs have an unquestionable value to our society. Thanks to medicines like morphine and OxyContin, patients can escape discomfort and feel normal, even good, while recovering from surgery. Yet those same drugs are a scourge on our society, addicting and even killing people who are unable to distinguish between a good feeling and a good result.

Good parents will tell their children that food is good but overeating is bad; that while sex is good, casual sex is harmful. Too much of a good thing is, well, a bad thing. Pleasure can be an instrument of temptation, a carrier of disease, or a mask for wrongdoing. There's no equation between what's pleasurable and what's best. Pleasure, by itself, is neither good nor good for you; in fact, it can be positively evil.

But most of us refuse to acknowledge that. Even less are we interested in finding some benefit in suffering.

THE VALUE OF PAIN

Clearly, it's possible for what feels good to produce a bad outcome. It's true also that what feels bad might sometimes lead to a good result. If the dirty little secret about pleasure is that it can hurt you, there's an equally well-kept secret about pain: it can help. That singularly unpopular view of the world happens to be the one found in Scripture and the one validated by common sense. Pain, unpleasant though it may be, can be put to good use.

Pain as Symptom

Hidden within your body is a network of nerves that have just one purpose: to feel pain. Pain is one way your body communicates with your mind, and that's a good thing. Pain begins with an electrical message in special pain receptors throughout your body. That message is transmitted through the spinal cord toward the brain. You become conscious of pain when your brain receives and interprets this electrical message.

Then you react.

Sometimes the reaction is involuntary. You don't have to think about whether or not to withdraw your hand from a hot stove. You just do it. Your brain sends an automatic message to the muscles near the source of the pain message, telling them to contract in order to evade the source of pain. The pain makes you jump.[5]

At other times, the response is voluntary, meaning that you must choose to take action to avoid pain. Many people can name the symptoms of a heart attack. All of them involve pain: chest pain, jaw pain, heartburn, pain in the upper back, shortness of breath, nausea. Most people who experience these symptoms consult a doctor. The pain itself keeps you alive in that it drives you to take lifesaving action.

That can be true spiritually as well as physically. C. S. Lewis made the well-known remark that "pain is God's megaphone to rouse a deaf world."[6] Lewis believed that God whispers to us in our pleasure but shouts to us in our pain. If so, God was in full voice in the Garden of Eden.

After Adam and Eve chose to disobey God's command in the Garden of Eden and eat the forbidden fruit, they felt a kind of spiritual pain, called guilt, and its cousin, shame. Knowing they had done wrong, they became afraid and hid themselves from God (Gen. 3:7–10). Their pain, in the form of guilt, did its job. It alerted them to a spiritual problem, their broken relationship with their Creator. When they tried to ignore the problem, first by hiding, then by blaming one another, God upped the ante by placing a curse on the world—a curse that included toil, pain in childbearing, and death.

When you stub your toe, the pain tells you to turn on a light. When you feel guilt, that spiritual discomfort should have the same effect, warning you to watch the way you're living.

We could wish for a life without pain, but would that be a good thing? In fact, some people do "enjoy" such an existence. Born with a rare condition known as *congenital analgesia*—the inability to feel pain—they usually die young from injuries they never feel, their bodies scarred from head to toe.[7] Because they cannot feel pain, they cannot live—or at least not well.

Others live without spiritual pain. The apostle Paul describes them in Rom. 1 as people who are oblivious to guilt or shame. Having ignored God and his attempts to communicate with them, they enter a downward spiral of humanistic philosophy, false worship, and sexual perversion. In the end, they become completely self-centered, oblivious to the effects of their actions on themselves or others (see Rom. 1:18–32). In a world plagued by evils like terrorism, sexually transmitted disease, drug addiction, violent crime, and the sexual abuse of children, we must conclude that Lewis is right. It's as if God screams from heaven, "Enough!"

Pain, at its most basic level, serves a vital purpose. It drives us to avoid danger and seek relief. But as it was in the Garden of Eden, so it is today. Most of us would rather ignore pain than be instructed by it. When suffering from a toothache, we'll do anything but go to a dentist. And when we feel guilt, shame, or remorse, we often ignore the very one who could alleviate the pain—God.

Pain as Discipline

Some readers of this book are old enough to remember when "time out" was a break in the action at a sporting event. In the days before children sued their parents, paternal discipline was accomplished with a device other than a chair—corporal punishment. Bare hands, belts, wooden spoons, and even hickory switches were applied to the backsides of wayward youngsters. Although the practice has been terribly abused, it was often effective. Fear of the belt extinguished thousands of cigarettes, halted numberless sibling rivalries, and sanitized countless conversations. Pain is an excellent motivator, and that makes it a useful tool for discipline.

Who knows that better than God?

About 3,500 years ago, God took his people to the woodshed for 40 years. After being rescued from slavery in Egypt, God's people, the Israelites, were an unruly bunch. Obstinate, argumentative, and demanding, they behaved more like spoiled children than liberated slaves. So God disciplined them (see Deut. 8:2–5). For 40 years he caused them to wander in the desert, where they experienced hunger and thirst. The exercise had a simple object: to teach obedience. God used pain in the form of hunger, thirst, and even disease to discipline his children.

Does God still do that? The Book of Hebrews gives a candid answer. Yes, God still disciplines his children.

> You have forgotten that word of encouragement that addresses you as sons: "My son, do not make light of the Lord's discipline, and do not lose heart when he rebukes you, because the Lord disciplines those he loves, and he punishes everyone he accepts as a son." Endure hardship as discipline; God is treating you as sons. For what son is not disciplined by his father? If you are not disciplined (and everyone undergoes discipline), then you are illegitimate children and not true sons. Moreover, we have all had human fathers who disciplined us and we respected them for it. How much more should we submit to the Father of our spirits and live! Our fathers disciplined us for a little while as they thought best; but God disciplines us for our good, that we may share in his holiness. No discipline seems pleasant at the time, but painful. Later on, however, it produces a harvest of righteousness and peace for those who have been trained by it (Heb. 12:5–11).

Mark Twain observed that a cat won't sit on a hot stove twice. The lesson of pain not lost on animals is often lost on humans. Like the Israelites, we would rather grumble about our circumstances than allow them to drive us toward God. Elisabeth Kübler Ross said, "There is no joy without hardship," and "When you learn your lessons, the pain goes away."[8] It's possible that we suffer as much as we do because we fail to ask the right questions of suffering, learn the lessons from it, and grow into the people God's intends for us to be.

Pain as Judgment

The legend holds that Sir Isaac Newton discovered the principle of gravity when, sitting under an apple tree, he was struck upon the head by a piece of falling fruit. I doubt it. Anyone as bright as this 17th-century mathematician and philosopher, who laid the groundwork for the modern discipline of physics and formulated the laws of motion, would have enough sense not to sit under an apple tree in the fall.

But either way, Newton did give expression to what we know as the Universal Law of Gravity, which states that every object in the universe attracts every other object. In other words, apples fall to the ground. Always. Everywhere. In all circumstances. It's the way the world works.

If that law were ever broken, if an apple ever fell up or if some people who jumped off tall buildings simply floated in the air, there would be chaos. What would the world be like if some airplanes did not descend when their pilots tried to land them or if basketball players who jumped into the air sometimes rose indefinitely? The world works only because some things are always true, always right, and always happen.

We have other laws besides the laws of motion. We have laws against murder, for example, and stealing, and in some jurisdictions, adultery. These are not merely our laws. They are laws sewn into the fabric of the universe by God himself. It was God who said "Do not murder," "Do not commit adultery," and "Do not steal" (Exod. 20:13–15).

Yet unlike the law of gravity, these laws are often broken. People commit murder, theft, and adultery every day. Can you imagine what the world would be like if those laws were never broken? In fact we can. We long for that world continually. It troubles us that guilty people go unpunished, and that unsettled feeling accounts for another of the questions about evil that we so often ask God: Why do people get away with wrongdoing? Why doesn't God punish those who inflict suffering on others?

Those questions are not new. More than 2,500 years ago, the prophet Jeremiah complained to God because he tolerated injustice (Jer. 20:7–18) as did the prophet Habakkuk, asking, "Why do you make me look at injustice? Why do you tolerate wrong?" (Hab. 1:3). In the time of the prophet Malachi, that identical complaint was widespread. Injustice was so common that many people concluded, "All who do evil are good in the eyes of the LORD, and he is pleased with them" They asked, "Where is the God of justice?" (Mal. 2:17).

What the prophets longed for was justice, and we hunger for it too. People should get what they deserve, we believe. And some people deserve to be punished.

It's ironic that we blame God for allowing us to suffer yet accuse him with equal venom when he does not inflict suffering on others. Our hunger for justice, whether we know it or not, is an acknowledgment that pain can be used for some positive purpose: to punish evil. Just as apples fall to the earth every time, so we long for murder, child abuse, stealing, and lying to be justly punished.

And that's exactly what God intends to do—all in good time.

ASKING THE RIGHT QUESTIONS

If it's true that pleasure is not an absolute good and that good can result from pain, then we spend most of our time asking the wrong questions about both. We're usually concerned with how to experience pleasure and avoid pain. We will go to great lengths to accomplish either goal. Yet pleasure is not an absolute good, to be sought in all circumstances; and pain is not an absolute evil, to be avoided at any cost. Either can destroy life, and either can enhance it.

No, we do not enjoy suffering, nor are we intended to. We are intended to endure it, to learn from it, and to grow in spite of—and sometimes because of it. Those who rush to escape all pain or, worse yet, ignore it, minimize, or merely lament it, miss a significant opportunity. Their suffering is truly useless, because they refuse to allow it any function in their lives.

God, as it turns out, is far less concerned about whether we're happy or miserable than he is with whether we're growing toward maturity. We worry about current circumstances— whether we're happy, comfortable, and enjoying life—and that leads us to spend most of our time wondering what feels right. A better question is this: *What is right?* We ask, *Why did this happen to me?* when we might better wonder, *What can I learn from it?*

For when we learn to enjoy pleasure rather than worship it, to accept pain rather than fear it, and to seek God in either circumstance, we're more likely to live lives that are truly good and not merely either comfortable or miserable. Then we will seek God in every circumstance, even suffering, and find him there. This is the abundant life that Jesus promised: that our days might be filled not merely with wealth or leisure or pleasure, but filled with meaning, filled with contentment, filled with purpose—filled with the knowledge of God.

QUESTIONS FOR REFLECTION

1. What circumstance most recently prompted you to wonder why God allows suffering?

2. When was the last time you got stung by pleasure— when you did something that promised a good feeling but resulted in pain? What, if anything, did you learn from that experience?

3. What do you think of the statement by C. S. Lewis that God whispers to us in our pleasure but shouts to us in our pain? What may God have been trying to tell you recently from the experience of either pleasure or pain?

4. Reflect on this statement by Elisabeth Kübler Ross: "There is no joy without hardship." Do you believe it? What joy may lie on the other side of a hardship that you have recently experienced? What might you have to do in order to experience that joy?

2

A PERFECT WORLD
THE COST OF FREEDOM

Why does life have to be this way?

We choose our joys and sorrows long
before we experience them.
—Kahlil Gibran, *Sand and Foam*

Rod Serling was the dark genius of television's early years. In 1959 he introduced a half-hour science fiction program that has become a staple of American culture. For five seasons *The Twilight Zone* ushered viewers into a fictional "fifth dimension" on Friday evenings at ten o'clock. With his trademark grim expression and smoldering cigarette, Serling introduced episodes in which ordinary people confronted surreal circumstances. Making use of a different setting and cast each week, the program explored fantastic what-if scenarios, often playing out the implications of a fantasy and demonstrating that having one's dream come true may be the worst thing that can happen. Such was the case on the evening of April 16, 1960, in an episode entitled "A Nice Place to Visit." As Serling himself might have said, consider the following:

A petty thief named Rocky Valentine is looting a pawnshop when he hears the sound of police sirens. Rocky tries to make a getaway but is cornered by policemen. When he refuses to surrender, they open fire. Suddenly a man dressed in white stands over Rocky, addressing him as "Mr. Valentine." The man introduces himself as Pip and says that his job is to be Rocky's guide, procuring for him whatever he wants in exchange for nothing.

Rocky is suspicious of the offer and tries an experiment. He demands money, and Pip produces a wad of 50-dollar bills. Still wary, Rocky follows the man to an expensive hotel suite where he notices a nameplate on the door reading "Henry Francis Valentine."

After being shown the master bedroom and offered a change of clothes, Rocky begins to question the mysterious man in white. Unable to believe that such good fortune could come without any price, Rocky finally becomes angry, draws his gun, and shoots Pip.

Nothing happens.

Then Rocky remembers the policemen and recalls that he himself had been shot. He concludes that he has died and gone to heaven. Now convinced that his luck will hold, the two-bit thug begins taking advantage of the situation. He asks for a million dollars and gets it. He demands a gorgeous woman, and one enters the room. He goes to a casino and begins playing the slot machines, hitting the jackpot every time. He returns to the hotel suite where the revelry continues at full tilt.

But one question nags at Rocky. Why would *he* be allowed into heaven?

As the good times wear on, Rocky plays a game of cards and wins every hand. He picks up a pool cue and begins a game, sinking all the balls on the first shot. Suddenly the endless good fortune becomes boring, and Rocky throws his companions out of the room. He confides to Pip that he's tired of this new life because there's no challenge. He wants adventure, danger, risk—he wants to feel alive. Finally he tells Pip that he shouldn't be here; he doesn't deserve what he's getting—he would rather go to hell.

"But, Sir," Pip replies, "where did you think you were?"

Would a perfect life really be perfect? Our blithe assumption is that a world in which there were no suffering, pain, or discomfort of any kind would be ideal.

But it wouldn't be.

I speak from experience—not mine but that of two distant relations: a great-great uncle named Adam, and his wife, Eve.

THE PERFECT WORLD

Thomas Aquinas believed that every evil has its basis in some good. "Evil cannot exist but in good," he wrote. "Sheer evil is impossible."[1] If that's true, then suffering itself owes its existence to some other, better thing. The fact that we experience pain, which is very bad, must be grounded in something else, which is very good. Does that sound infeasible?

It isn't.

The fact that we suffer, that we feel pain, that we experience hurt and heartache and guilt and fear and terror has its genesis in the crowning achievement of God's creation, the best of all good things that he made: human freedom.

The perfect world that we so often long for did exist at one time. When God created the world, he placed the first human pair, Adam and Eve, in a garden called Eden.[2] Life there was perfect, or it seemed to be. The two had all they needed, knew no toil, and enjoyed intimate fellowship with each other and with God. There was no pain, no death, no hunger, no tears, and perhaps best of all, no time clock.

There was, however, one rule. God forbade them to eat from one of the two trees in the middle of the garden, the tree of the knowledge of good and evil. To do so would bring a curse of death. Adam and Eve both knew the rule, and both obeyed it.

This is the perfect world that most people long for, and it was ours. There was no pain, no suffering, no death, nothing but endless days in which to enjoy being alive.

And there was one other thing in this perfect world: possibility.

The Possibility

There are some 633 laws in the Old Testament. There are even more laws on the books of most jurisdictions. We have laws against nearly every harmful behavior. It's against the law to commit murder, rape, or incest. Of course, people do these things anyway. In many places it's unlawful to do a host of offensive things such as run a red light, drive without a seatbelt, or litter. Again, people frequently do these things in spite of the laws against them.

There are some things, however, that are not against the law, even though they might be immoral or dangerous. It's not against the law to travel backward through time. It violates no ordinance to transform oneself into a chicken. There are no zoning restrictions that prohibit building condominiums on the sun. Absurd? Precisely. There are no laws against any of these things because they're absurd. In fact, they're impossible. Laws always deal with possible, even probable, behavior. The mere existence of a law implies the possibility that it may be broken. A law does not prevent action—it prescribes the action's consequence.

So when God declared a law against eating fruit from the tree of knowledge, he admitted the possibility that it could be eaten. He disclosed that human beings have the ability to act in a way contrary to his own will. God's creatures were not forced to behave in the way he chose for them or the way he himself would behave. Adam and Eve were not bound to obey God—or else why would he state the law? Adam and Eve were free. God created them that way.

And God created something along with human freedom: the consequence for disobedience. When God further decreed that to eat the forbidden fruit would result in death, he allowed the possibility that people would die. And that was necessary, for if there were no consequence for the behavior, the act would be meaningless. As Shakespeare said, "There's small choice in rotten apples."³ If all our choices were the same, if eating the fruit were no different from not eating, if walking off a cliff were just the same as falling asleep, if making love produced no result different from committing murder, then would any action have value? If Adam's choices had no consequence, they would not have been free choices. If there had been no possibility of death, then life would have held no value. The consequence of an action reveals its value or harm.

What's the point?

Simply this: God created a world of possibility, a world with the potential for both obedience and disobedience, both pleasure and pain. When he made the world, when he made you, he realized that human beings—you—could suffer, and would.

But he did it anyway.

More than likely, you would have done it too.

The Alternative

What can go wrong will go wrong, according to Murphy's Law. Had Murphy been a theologian, he might have said, "Where sin is possible, sin is probable." Eve ate the fruit. Adam ate it too. In a sense, we've been eating it ever since, constantly choosing to disobey God's commands—which have become rather more numerous. Why did they do it? We can trace their rationale in Gen. 3:4–6:

> "You will not surely die," the serpent said to the woman. "For God knows that when you eat of it your eyes will be opened, and you will be like God, knowing good and evil."
>
> When the woman saw that the fruit of the tree was good for food and pleasing to the eye, and also desirable for gaining wisdom, she took some and ate it. She also gave some to her husband, who was with her, and he ate it.

Eve wanted to be like God. Adam wanted to be like Eve. Those may be the most basic rationale for every person's sin. We disobey God because we believe it will improve our lives in some way or because we don't want to be left out. Adam and Eve were given one boundary, and they couldn't resist crossing it. Though it meant death, they reached for the forbidden fruit, and we continue to suffer the consequences of that one selfish act.[4] With every cancer diagnosis, every criminal conviction, every broken heart, even every stubbed toe, we're reminded that human beings have chosen their own way in the wide world; we would rather die than live within limits.

But why did God allow such senseless behavior? Why did he create a world in which such awful results were possible? Why did he create the possibility, indeed the inevitability, that people would disobey him and suffer as a result?

Here's a better question: what was the alternative? If God had created a world in which there were no possibilities, what would that world be like? What would our lives be like if there were no potential for pain? Would there be any joy? Achievement? Satisfaction? Love?

Aquinas's logic, if correct, must work in both directions. If every evil thing is rooted in a good thing, then every good thing has some connection, some counterpoint, in evil. If we were unable to hate, we would be unable to love. If there were no potential for sorrow, there could be no joy. If there were no pain, there could be no pleasure. If there were no consequences, there could be no rewards. If there were no potential for pain, Adam and Eve would have been free in the garden as a bird is free in its cage. They would have been free to go to the mailbox but never to cross the road, free to eat their vegetables, make their beds, and brush their teeth, but never free—in fact, never able—to wonder, explore, invent, risk, or dare. They would have obeyed God without thought, without choice, without conscience, without love. They would have been something other than human beings, created in the image of God, able to exercise the power of choice.[5]

Would we enjoy living in a world in which everything was perfect, where there was no pain, no suffering, not the slightest discomfort whatsoever? In fact, we did have such a life once. And we disliked it so much that we let it go. For neither we nor God was willing to accept the condition for that particular brand of the "good life"—the absence of the human will.

For the choice is never between a world in which there's no sickness and a world in which people die of cancer, or between a life of perfect ease and a life of constant labor. The choice is between a world of suffering and a world of slavery, between a deterministic, meaningless existence and a life filled with possibility. In his sovereign wisdom, God concluded that a world with both freedom and suffering is preferable to a world without either.

A World of Possibility

According to some philosophies, human beings are little more than computer chips, animated by electrons perhaps, but having no authentic existence. Every action they take, from committing murder to falling in love to choosing corn flakes over scrambled eggs, is carefully prescribed by some outside source—fate, or chance, or God.

Few people relish that belief. It contradicts everything we feel about ourselves and goes against the tenor of Scripture. Deep down, we know that our choices *do* matter because we know that *we* matter. We're not machines or robots or electronic impulses coursing through a computer grid. We're human beings, created in the image of God, having the ability to make meaningful, if limited, choices.

And if that means that God allows us to suffer, it means also that he allows us to grow. If we can reject God, feel pain, suffer, victimize others, and become victims ourselves, we can also accept God's grace, enjoy a relationship with him, and have a positive effect on the world around us. We live in a world of possibility.

Meaning

Human beings are free in a limited sense. We have the freedom that God allows us, but that's not absolute freedom. We cannot create *ex nihil*, from nothing, as he can. Although we can reproduce, we cannot create life apart from the bio-mechanism that he has ordained. We can apply our knowledge to the art of medicine, but we cannot heal as God heals, by our word. We are bound by time and space; he is not. In his sovereignty God has permitted to us a measure of freedom, including the ability to make meaningful moral choices. Primarily, that means we're free to reject his grace in our lives, and we're free to accept it.

Yet within even that limited range of choices, we enjoy something that no plant, no animal, and no angel can fathom: meaning. The things we do *really matter*.

Each day we're faced with choices—what to say, how to think, whom to speak to; whether to work, lie in bed, curse, comfort, eat, exercise, lie, steal, or worship. We decide. And there are consequences for those choices. It does matter to others, to our families, to ourselves, and ultimately to God, whether we comfort people or kill them. And it's precisely because it does matter that there's pain in the world, for without it our choices would be meaningless, and so would our lives.

Change

Trees grow. Dogs grow. Cats grow. But none of them change. A tree can grow tall, but it can't become anything other than a tree. A dog can't grow up to become a bear. As the saying goes, a leopard can't change its spots.

But *we* can change.

The miracle of God's grace is that we can become different than we were (see 2 Cor. 5:17). People who were once alienated from God can become his friends (see Eph. 2:19). Those who used to do the most wicked things can be changed, their hearts can be purified, they can grow to become like God. We, who used to behave selfishly, can change to become holy, godly, and pure in heart. The God who created us with the ability to choose can also strengthen our will so that we're enabled to finally make the right choices that seem so elusive. The apostle Peter wrote,

> His divine power has given us everything we need for life and godliness through our knowledge of him who called us by his own glory and goodness. Through these he has given us his very great and precious promises, so that through them you may participate in the divine nature and escape the corruption in the world caused by evil desires (2 Pet. 1:3–4).

None of that would happen in a world where there was no possibility, where there was no potential for suffering. Because we feel pain, we can grow. That means the things that grieve you most about yourself and about the world—your own sin, the suffering of others, injustice, hunger, prejudice—can be changed.

Reward

It's axiomatic in the world of business that one must risk money in order to make money. Nothing ventured, nothing gained, so the saying goes. Without risk, there's no possibility of reward. This principle holds in a spiritual sense as well. We have something to lose. The possibility of eternal suffering exists. Hell is real (see Matt. 13:49–50; 2 Thess. 1:8–9; Rev. 21:8), and so is heaven (see 1 Pet. 1:3–4; Rev. 21:1, 4). We have something to lose and something to gain.

The apostle Paul makes a direct connection between our

present life, fraught with suffering, and the eternal reward that we'll soon enjoy because of our faith in Christ. He writes,

Our light and momentary troubles are achieving for us an eternal glory that far outweighs them all. So we fix our eyes not on what is seen, but on what is unseen. For what is seen is temporary, but what is unseen is eternal (2 Cor. 4:17–18).

In Paul's mind, the fact that we suffer now only adds to the glory that we'll experience in heaven. Grief, pain, heartbreak, loss, illness—these things will disappear someday. The fact that we experience them now heightens anticipation for the life to come. Because we suffer, we have hope. Because we have something to lose, we have something to gain.

Fellowship

Let's go back to the Garden for one last look at the ideal life there. Just after Adam and Eve ate the forbidden fruit, we get this lingering glimpse of the life they once enjoyed:

Then the man and his wife heard the sound of the LORD God as he was walking in the garden in the cool of the day, and they hid from the LORD God among the trees of the garden. But the LORD God called to the man, "Where are you?" (Gen. 3:8–9).

Apparently God was in the habit of taking evening walks in the Garden with Adam and Eve. And when they didn't appear as usual, God went looking for them.

Incredible!

To which other of God's creatures does he call, "Where are you?" How often in the Bible do we see God taking a stroll with elephants or chimpanzees or even angels? Yet God had a relationship, a friendship, with these human beings.

How is that possible? It is possible precisely because they were created with freedom. They were not forced to walk with God—they chose to. They did not answer his call from reflex or instinct—they desired his company (and later feared it). God could hold conversation with these two creatures because he created them different from the rest. He gave them freedom: the freedom to experience pain, and the freedom to experience a relationship with him.

That relationship is still possible, and God still desires it. He still calls out to people, "Where are you?" always hoping for a response. We can hear his voice and hide as Adam did, or we can hear his voice and answer, "Here I am." God has given us that freedom, the freedom to relate to him as a friend.

It would have been easier in some ways if God had created us as animals, guided only by instinct, or as computers, able to do only what we're programmed to do. We would have no responsibility, no fear of failure, no pain, no remorse. Yet, as Helen Keller observed, "Avoiding danger is no safer in the long run than outright exposure. Life is either a daring adventure, or nothing." In a safe, painless life, we would have no freedom, no possibility, no change, no growth. Worst of all, we would have no meaningful relationship with him. God placed the door of possibility in the Garden of Eden, and he left the door unlocked.

THE OPEN DOOR

Jim Carey is one of the few actors of the present generation to attempt both comedy and drama in the same career—or in the same film. He did so in a delightful film entitled *The Truman Show*, a surprisingly adept parable of divine sovereignty and human freedom.

The setting is the chirpy little town of Seahaven, an idyllic island community in southern California. Truman Burbank is a happy-go-lucky insurance salesman, blissfully married and without a care—until he begins to suspect that his life might not be what it appears to be.

What Truman does not know is that every day of his life has been carefully scripted and is broadcast as a television program. His wife, boss, best friend, and even parents, are all actors. The town of Seahaven is a gigantic set. Without realizing it, Truman has been the star of a top-rated reality show since the day of his birth. Christof, the mad genius who produces the show, exercises absolute control over Truman's environment, carefully orchestrating every event from playground games to high school graduation to falling in love. Even the sun in Seahaven rises and sets on cue.

But Truman longs to venture beyond Seahaven. Fueled by dreams of sailing to the far-away Fiji islands, Truman begins to explore. As he does, he realizes that he's not able to go wherever he chooses. He tries to enter an office building, only to find that it's mysteriously closed in the middle of the day. He tries to drive out of Seahaven, only to find every road jammed with traffic—all produced on cue from the omnipresent Christof.

Finally Truman sneaks out at night and commandeers a sailboat. He ventures out to sea, not realizing that the "ocean" is really a moat within the dome of the show's enormous set. As Truman sails closer and closer to the edge of his world, Christof faces a decision. Will he produce a storm that drives Truman back to shore, forcing him to live within the protective confines of the television set? Or will he allow Truman to set his own course, to follow his dream, to be free?

Realizing at last that he cannot contain the spirit of a human being, Christof allows Truman to sail on. Minutes later, Truman bumps into the enormous dome that encompasses Seahaven, discovers a door to the greater world beyond, and walks away—from paradise.

When faced with the choice between living a "perfect" but perfectly scripted life and living a life with both adventure and risk, both possibility and pain, Truman chose freedom. When faced with the choice between keeping his "child" safe but captive and allowing him to be vulnerable but free, Christof chose to let him go.

God made the same choice with Adam and Eve, and he makes the same choice with you. We endure pain because we enjoy possibility. We experience suffering because we exercise freedom. We suffer consequences because we make meaningful choices. God allowed his first children to break through the shell of paradise and walk away. Though it meant their deaths, he would not keep them sheltered against their will.

That door of possibility remains open. Adam and Eve, and every human being since, chose to walk through it. And God let them.

Would you rather he had locked the door?

QUESTIONS FOR REFLECTION

1. Why do you think some people prefer to believe in a controlling God, one who scripts every aspect of their existence, rather than a God who allows freedom?

2. If God created a world in which both human freedom and its consequences are possible, then who is ultimately responsible for the existence of suffering?

3. Of the things you've suffered lately, for which do you bear some direct responsibility? For which are you the victim of someone else's actions?

4. Do you think it's possible to use your freedom to do what's right rather than disobeying God frequently? Do you think you could live that way now? Do you think we'll live that way in heaven?

5. Are you optimistic or pessimistic about the future?

3

THE NEED TO KNOW
FAITH BEYOND REASON

Why would God do this to me?

Who is this that darkens my counsel
with words without knowledge?
—Job 38:2

I almost never want to hurt people, but I would have slapped that woman if I could have reached her. Fortunately, a hundred miles of telephone line stood between us. She had called our home a day after my wife suffered a miscarriage, offering unwanted advice on the reason for human suffering—ours in particular.

The word *miscarriage* offers an inadequate description of what happened. The tiny child my wife had conceived had died. To remove its remains, a surgeon had to blindly probe her body with a sharp instrument. For a few short weeks we had joyfully expected the first addition to our family. Two minutes in the doctor's examining room had done away with that hope.

"The fetus is dead—we'll have to remove it."

Four hours later, we left the hospital with nothing but the nagging question that lingers in the mind of every grieving parent: Why did God allow this? If he really can do anything, he could have kept that child alive. But he didn't. Why?

While my wife slept upstairs, an acquaintance called to offer sympathy. With it, she proffered a dime-store rationale for why bad things happen to good people. "Will you tell your wife something?" she demanded.

"Um—sure."

"I want you to tell her that God always has a reason, and sometimes nature's way is best." Then she hung up.

It wasn't hard to connect the dots. God let your baby die because it was a freak. *How reassuring!* Look on the bright side; you probably would have been stuck with a deformed child. *Isn't that comforting?* You should be relieved; God spared you a lifetime of suffering. *How thoughtful of you to say so!*

I hung up the phone in disgust, glad the woman was not at arm's length. *Is this the God we serve,* I wondered, *one who blights children, then exterminates them out of mercy?*

In the weeks that followed, I heard that woman's advice repeated many times. Often some well-meaning believer would touch me on the elbow and whisper, "Remember—all things work together for good." Usually the couplet was completed with some version of the Mother-Nature-knows-best refrain. God killed your baby rather than let it suffer. See—isn't God good? I learned to smile patiently and say nothing.

Yet in spite of myself, I began to wonder whether it might be true. I sensed that if there were some cause, some good result that could be obtained from the loss, it wouldn't hurt so much. If I could be sure that God did have some good reason for what he had done, it would be easier to accept what happened.

Two years went by. M0y wife conceived again and gave birth to a beautiful, healthy baby boy. Another year passed, and she became pregnant once more, giving birth to our first daughter. We were elated.

But again, our happy dream was dissolved by a few words from the doctor's mouth.

"Your daughter has a rare genetic disorder. It has produced some birth defects."

"How bad?"

"About as bad as I've seen."

This time there had been no miscarriage. The ailing child whom God had "mercifully" allowed to die three years earlier was now born alive. After an anxiety-filled week in the neonatal intensive care unit, we brought Laurinda home, where we cared for her for five months. She required constant attention, special feedings, oxygen, antiseizure medication, and a host of other nursing treatments. We ate little, slept less, and worried continuously. Our own health began to fail.

Oddly, many of the same people who had been convinced that God in his mercy had allowed our first child to die were now sure there was some noble purpose in Laurinda being born with a critical illness. Their rationale was exactly the opposite of before.

God knew that this precious angel needed a loving family. That's why he picked you. *Who am I, Dirty Harry? . . . every dirty job that comes along?*

Think of the way you'll be able to help others, now that you know what it's like to have a sick child. *So this is Hell Week for parents . . . the few, the proud?*

It was the B-side of God's mercy. Job's comforters simply flipped the record over and played their pious answers in reverse. When our child died before birth, it was because God wanted to spare us suffering. When our child was born with a severe illness, it was because God wanted us to experience suffering. Like a dog chasing its tail, their reasons followed an odd circle, never quite latching on to the goal—to find logic in pain.

It has been 15 years since Laurinda flickered to life and died. No reason that anyone offered for the death of a child made sense to me then. None makes sense to me now. I don't say that God had no reason for allowing suffering in her life or in mine—I simply have no idea what it might be. And anyone who tells me that he or she does know is a fool. For only a fool would claim to know what God has refused to say.

THE SEARCH FOR REASON

Perhaps the most misused verse in Scripture is Rom. 8:28— "We know that in all things God works for the good of those who love him, who have been called according to his purpose." That means, simply, that God is at work in our lives through every circumstance. Ultimately he will achieve our eternal salvation in spite of what we may experience in the meantime. Although we suffer now, God still loves us, and heaven awaits. Nothing can change that. Neither this one verse nor its context (Rom. 8:18–39) says anything about the *reason* for suffering. The point of the entire passage is that we can count on God's love for us no matter what.

Yet armed with this verse, countless believers have set off on safari, intrepidly hunting for that one "good reason" God allowed a specific instance of evil. The trophies are exotic, to say the least:

- God let your son die so you would know how to comfort other people.
- God made you sick to keep you humble.
- God hasn't healed your wife because he wants one more person to pray for her.
- God created AIDS to punish homosexuals.

The portrait that emerges is of a bizarre, vindictive, changeable God, one who heals or doesn't heal, inflicts pain or bestows wealth based on the most arbitrary rationale. But at least there is one, and we take comfort in that. More than anything, we want to see some reason for what we suffer. If our suffering cannot be relieved, if we must endure this pain, then please, God—let there be a reason.

But God seldom reveals the reason for any of his actions.

For better or worse, he keeps his rationale mostly to himself. There are two good reasons for that. One is that he doesn't owe us an answer. And the other is that even if he gave it, we probably wouldn't understand.

GOD ABOVE REASON

Our craving for reason is rooted in some of the most basic human needs and fears. We long for stability and predictability. We fear change. We crave control. If we can understand why things happen, we can better cope with them. Understanding is our key to acceptance. When we understand what God does, we find it easier to trust him.

It's always easiest to trust God when he does what seems right—at least to us. For example, it was wicked of Pharaoh to oppress the Hebrew people in Egypt. So when God sent Moses to deliver them, God did a good thing. Everyone could see that, including legendary Hollywood producer Cecil B. DeMille. *The Ten Commandments* is a classic movie precisely because it adheres to our preconceived standard of right and wrong. The good guys win in the end, and the villains are made to pay. We have no problem with that.

But what happens when God *doesn't* adhere to the standard we know and accept? What happens when we don't understand the rules God is playing by, or, worse yet, we *do* understand them and God still doesn't appear to be fair? What happens when the good guys *don't* win? What happens when good people suffer and the guilty go unpunished? How do we make sense of God when he allows the death of a child? What if, heaven forbid, God even commanded it?

In fact, he did. You can read the story in Gen. 22.

The Standard for Better

The story of Abraham and Isaac is a story that takes us way outside the boundaries that we know as normal or even moral.

The story begins with an event that so greatly contradicts the laws of nature that it must be called a miracle: the birth of Isaac.

Abraham and Sarah were childless well into their old age when God promised them a son.[1] Years later, Isaac was born. In that act, God went outside the norm; he broke one of his own rules for life. Babies simply are not born to postmenopausal women, but he made an exception for Sarah.

Interestingly, nobody asked why. No one thought to ask whether God might be good or fair by giving a baby to a childless couple. God broke one of his own rules, and no one thought it was wrong.

Typically, we don't question God when he does as we wish. Divine healing, for example, is not "normal." In the world God created, people who have a terminal illness will die. But when they don't, we're glad. The prevention of a traffic accident may interrupt the law of cause and effect, but when God miraculously prevents harm, we think of it as a good thing. When God behaves in a manner that we think right, we don't question him—even if he seems to break one of his own rules.

The Standard for Worse

Fast forward eight or ten years. Isaac is now a healthy, growing boy. In one of those I-can't-believe-you-really-said-that moments, God spoke directly to Abraham and gave him an unmistakable command: "Take your son, your only son, Isaac, whom you love, and go to the region of Moriah. Sacrifice him there as a burnt offering on one of the mountains I will tell you about" (Gen. 22:2).

God again broke one of his own rules. This time he ordered a human sacrifice, a murder. That's wrong. It's wrong now, and it was wrong then. God had already said so.[2] First, God established a standard of conduct—a moral, not a physical, law—and then he broke it.

Even now, defenses for God are probably boiling up in your

mind. *But this was different. God never intended to go through with it. It was only a test. God stopped Abraham before he killed the boy. He just wanted to see if Abraham would obey.*

All of that is true. But the command was still "wrong" by the standard God himself had set. There's no defense for this act—not one we can understand. According to all we know, God violated his own moral code. He did it not to heal or to prevent injury; that we could easily accept. The command was to kill, and that's wrong—as far as we know.

Why would God do that?

A Higher Standard

I've never met a parent who hasn't broken his or her word to a child. Bad parents give their word carelessly and break it capriciously. But even good parents will break their word on occasion. That's because some things are even more important than honoring a promise. A child's well-being, for example, is more important than a trip to the fair. A good parent will renege on a promised outing if the child has a temperature of 102. "But you promised" is the child's certain complaint. How can a four-year-old understand the relative value of good health compared to cotton candy? How can a child understand the conditions implicit in any statement by a parent—if you're well, if there's no tornado, if the car doesn't break down, if I'm not required to work overtime, if the creek doesn't rise. The analogy, facile perhaps, illustrates the principle in Scripture best stated by the prophet Isaiah:

"My thoughts are not your thoughts, neither are your ways my ways," declares the LORD. "As the heavens are higher than the earth, so are my ways higher than your ways and my thoughts than your thoughts" (Isa. 55:8–9).

The apostle Paul in typically grand style echoes this same thought and hints at another:

Oh, the depth of the riches of the wisdom and knowledge of God! How unsearchable his judgments, and his paths beyond tracing out! "Who has known the mind of the Lord? Or who has been his counselor?" "Who has ever given to God, that God should repay him?" For from him and through him and to him are all things. To him be the glory forever! Amen (Rom. 11:33–36).

God knows more than we do. There's no comparison between his mind and ours. As with any parent and child, his actions will sometimes seem puzzling, capricious, or even wrong. But they're not. They're simply in accord with a higher standard, his own.

The issue here is not God's character but his greatness. We look at what God has done or failed to do and ask why. We wonder, *Is God really good? Can he really be trusted if he behaves contrary to reason?* We want God's behavior always to fit snugly within the confines of our understanding. But what if it did? What kind of God would he be? What kind of parent would never take any action that his two-year-old would not approve of? What kind of God would never act except according to the will of his own creatures? It would be a small god indeed who was no bigger than the human mind.

And it would be small faith indeed that trusted God no further than he could be seen. It requires no faith at all to trust God when he does what we wish. It takes tremendous faith to trust God when he does or fails to do things that we don't understand. It requires even greater faith to trust God when he does things that appear to violate our idea of what is good or even acceptable conduct.

Abraham had that faith. He trusted God first when he promised a child—something contrary to reason but very good. Abraham trusted God also when he demanded the child's life—something contrary to both reason and conscience. Abraham was prepared to believe that God could allow—even demand—something awful, something painful beyond words, the death of his only son, and still be good. Abraham trusted God beyond his ability to understand him.

Will you?

THE ULTIMATE QUESTION

Still there is the question: *Why?* Amazingly, Abraham did not ask it. But others have. Job was one. And what Job discovered, like so many before and since, is that *Why?* is a question God nearly always refuses to answer.

The Question

Job was a righteous man. He's described in the Bible as "blameless and upright" (Job 1:1). He always did what was right. Yet in another of those I-can't-believe-God-did-that moments, Satan asked for permission to test Job's faith by inflicting misfortune on him—and God agreed! First Job's wealth and his children were destroyed by natural disaster and war; then Job himself was afflicted with painful sores all over his body.

That shocking opener sets up the remainder of Job's story, which is a series of arguments between Job and his "comforters." Although neither Job nor his friends know about the deal made by Satan and God, they all have theories about why Job, an unquestionably righteous man, is suffering. Job's friends insist that he must have done some wrong, some sin, for which he's being punished by God. Job insists that he's innocent and echoes the same refrain throughout: *Why has God done this to me?*

Some version of Job's thesis runs through the mind of every person who suffers: *I've done nothing to deserve this. Why would God do this to me?* We become indignant, even angry, at the presence of pain in our lives, and we call for an accounting from God. We demand to know why.

The Answer

When Jesus was placed on trial before Herod, he stood

mute (see Luke 23:9). He would not dignify that false king's accusations or satisfy his idle curiosity. When some Pharisees and teachers of the law asked Jesus to validate his identity by performing some miraculous sign, he refused (see Matt. 12:38–39). By doing so, Jesus demonstrated one of the basic principles that govern our interaction with God: he doesn't owe us anything. He'll speak when he chooses and remain silent when he desires. He's not obliged to make a reply to any of our questions, even *why*.

Does that sound harsh? God's reply to Job was even sterner.

After Job and his companions had exhausted themselves in argument, conjecturing on the nature of God and the reasons behind his behavior, God himself spoke. His statement was perhaps different from what Job expected.

> Then the LORD answered Job out of the storm. He said:
> "Who is this that darkens my counsel with words without knowledge? Brace yourself like a man; I will question you, and you shall answer me" (Job 38:1–3).

What followed was a lengthy interrogation in which God questioned Job's knowledge on every subject from the details of creation to the placement of the stars to the flight path of an eagle. *What do you know about the world,* God demanded, *that you would dare to question the way I run it?*

There was more.

God then took aim at Job's assertion—implicit within the very question *Why?*—that God had been unfair. "Would you discredit my justice?" God asked. "Would you condemn me to justify yourself?" (40:8). Finally, God zeroed in on the heart of the matter, asking the rhetorical question that Paul echoes centuries later: "Who has a claim against me that I must pay?" (41:11). There it is—the question that perhaps only God has the right to ask those who suffer and in that suffering question the honor of the God who allows it. For after all, what does

God owe *any* of us? For what reason should he give an accounting to us for the things he does?

The naked, unattractive, unavoidable truth is this: God doesn't have to justify his behavior, not to us, not to anyone. That's the prerogative of being God.

After God had spoken, Job came to realize what Abraham seemed implicitly to know. The issue is not God's character, but his greatness. If God were obliged to answer our demands, to satisfy our complaints, to rectify all that we see as wrong in the world, then how great a god would he be? Our relationship with God is not a contract between equal parties. He is not obliged to do as we see fit.

"Surely I spoke of things I did not understand," Job concluded, "things too wonderful for me to know" (42:3). Job admitted, finally, what every sufferer eventually comes to see: God doesn't have to give a reason for allowing us to suffer. And even if he gave one, we probably wouldn't understand.

The Silence

Unlike Job, many of us receive no response at all, not even chastisement, when we wonder why we're suffering. And silence can be a deafening thing. We hate it so much that we fill every minute of our lives with noise from television sets, computers, car radios, and CD players. When God doesn't answer, we babble and jabber to each other, we consult experts, we badger God for answers, and we invent them when he fails to respond. It's difficult to suffer in silence.

Job, in spite of his impertinent questioning, provides our model for coping with unexplained suffering. His life demonstrates that the real question concerning suffering is not why God allows it but how we'll respond to it. At the onset of his troubles, Job made two statements that form a towering pillar of strength for anyone faced with undeserved pain: "Shall we accept good from God, and not trouble?" Job asked (2:10).

"Naked I came from my mother's womb, and naked I will depart. The LORD gave and the LORD has taken away; may the name of the LORD be praised" (1:21).

Though he may not reveal his rationale, God certainly has one. As Paul so movingly reminds us in Rom. 8, God always has our ultimate good in mind, regardless of present circumstances. God is good—thoroughly, completely, totally good. And his love for us is unquestionable. In the end, all reasons will be revealed, all pain finally understood, all questions answered at long last.

In the meantime, the challenge of suffering is not to find reasons but to find faith, to trust God not because of what we know but in spite of what we don't know.

We suffer. Does that mean that God is not good? Does that mean that life is not worth living? Does that mean that our existence is futile or pointless?

No, in all these things we are more than conquerors through him who loved us. For I am convinced that neither death nor life, neither angels nor demons, neither the present nor the future, nor any powers, neither height nor depth, nor anything else in all creation, will be able to separate us from the love of God that is in Christ Jesus our Lord (Rom. 8:37–39).

And that's the one thing of which we can be absolutely sure.

BLESSED BE THE NAME

I now have two wonderful children. My son, Uriah, is smart as a whip and healthy as a horse. He has been a perfect delight to me every day of his life. My second daughter, Lydia, was born about two years after Laurinda's death. She is intelligent, attractive, and talented. Other than a bad case of chicken pox, there's never been a thing wrong with her.

Oddly, no one has ever thought it necessary to volunteer an explanation for their health. No well-meaning saint has ever laid a warm hand on my shoulder and whispered, "Now you must remember—God always has a reason for what he does. He gave you two healthy children because . . ."

We find it perfectly plausible when God does what we want. When he doesn't, we feel compelled to invent some defense, to offer some reason for his behavior, to contort his actions to fit within our limited understanding so we can say, "There—you see? God really *is* good, once you understand him." But it's no more possible to understand God than to train a cat. It's foolish pride that makes us think otherwise, that makes us believe we can bind God with the thread of reason or contain him within the narrow walls of the human mind.

Frankly, I prefer God as an independent thinker. What good would be a god who sits on command or meekly retreats to his cage when the whip of logic is cracked overhead?

Why did my wife miscarry? Why did Laurinda die? Why are Uriah and Lydia so bright and healthy? Why did God allow in my life the specific combination of pain and delight that he did?

I don't pretend to know. I know only that the Lord gave, and the Lord has taken away.

Blessed be the name of the Lord.

QUESTIONS FOR REFLECTION

1. What problem, loss, or suffering causes you to ask *Why?*

2. How can you tell the difference between understanding God's will through his Word and manufacturing reasons to explain a tragedy?

3. How do you react to unanswered questions? How will it affect your faith if you are not able to discover answers to your questions about pain?

4. Do you think God could provide answers to all our questions? If so, why would he choose not to?

4

A QUESTION OF JUSTICE
MERCY, PATIENCE, AND CHANCE

Why does God allow innocent people to suffer?

Use every man after his desert and
who should 'scape whipping?
—William Shakespeare, *Hamlet*, Act 2, Scene 2

The story is set against the breathtaking backdrop of the Rocky Mountains, near the close of the 19th century. By the thousands, Americans have heeded Horace Greeley's advice to "Go West, young man," and the fabled Wild West is fast becoming a memory. Outposts have become towns, towns have become cities, and the once-expansive prairie is slowly being devoured by ranches, fences, and farms. Meanwhile, a few independent spirits cling to a vanishing way of life, driving their herds of cattle across the high prairie, ever in search of fresh grazing land.

Open Range is a story of freedom and forgiveness eloquently dramatized by filmmaker Kevin Costner. It stars the venerable Robert Duvall as Boss Spearman, a craggy old cattleman who leads a tiny group of cowboys, free grazers, who claim the legal right to drive their herd on any open ground. The always-likeable Costner plays Charlie Waite, Boss's right-hand man and surrogate son. Mose Harrison, a brawny, good-natured blacksmith of a man, rides with them, as does "Button," a 16-year-old orphan with no other home than the open range. They camp for the night near the burgeoning town of Harmonville just before a summer thunderstorm sweeps over the prairie. The violent storm touches off a chain of events that destroys their little family and leaves Boss brooding over the question that troubles every person who suffers unjustly: *What kind of God would allow innocent people to suffer?*

After the storm clears, Mose rides into town to replenish supplies. There he meets up with some cowhands who work for Denton Baxter, a ruthless rancher who controls most of the land in the region and despises free grazers. Baxter's men brutally beat Mose, then have him jailed. Boss wins Mose's release but knows that Baxter will soon come after them all. Realizing that his herd, his fortune, and his very way of life are at stake, Boss leaves Button and the injured Mose to defend the herd while he and Charlie ride out to surprise Baxter's men, hoping to forestall their attack.

But while Boss and Charlie intimidate four would-be bushwhackers into turning back, a second group savagely attacks the herd, scattering the cattle, gravely wounding Button and leaving Mose dead on the prairie.

Boss and Charlie return to camp and are appalled by what they find. Tending the wounded Button through the night, they nurse thoughts of revenge. In the morning, they determine to head back to Harmonville, find a doctor for Button, and mete justice upon their enemies. Before they do, the taciturn cowboys hold an impromptu funeral for their friend. Standing beside the gravesite, Charlie searches for a way to consummate a proper burial. "It'd be right to say some words," he observes.

Boss's reply barely contains the anger and helplessness he feels over this senseless act of cruelty and gives voice to the emotions of many who have suffered not pain but injustice. Boss says, "You want to speak with the man upstairs—go on and do it. I'll stand right here and listen, hat in hand. But I ain't talking. And I'll be holdin' a grudge for him letting this befall a sweet kid like Mose."

A COMMON COMPLAINT

Boss's irreverent remark voices an attitude held by nearly everyone who witnesses suffering: *it's not fair.* When innocent people are abused, it's worse than painful; it's unjust. Therefore, we reason, God must be unjust for allowing it.

The notion is at least half right; for it *is* true that God allows suffering. He's responsible for everything that happens in the world, both good and bad. Who else could be? You? Me? Satan? If God is any God at all, he must be answerable for all that happens on his watch. If there were anything beyond God's control, then he would not be omnipotent.

That is one clear lesson from the book of Job. In the Bible's central lesson on suffering, we see that Satan must ask God's permission in order to inflict suffering upon Job. "Very well, then," God says to Satan, "he is in your hands; but you must spare his life" (Job 2:6). It's not Satan or Job or fate or gremlins or bad luck that's ultimately responsible for the fact that Job suffers. It's God.

If so, then Boss Spearman at least took his grievance to the right place. And he was not the first to do so. Throughout the Bible godly people give voice to a similar complaint.

Jeremiah was called by God to be a prophet. Prophets never have an easy task, and Jeremiah's was no exception. He lived in a time when his nation was complacent. Fat and happy, they had no interest in Jeremiah's calls for repentance or forecasts of judgment. Feeling as if he were the only person alive who felt the tension between what is and what should be, Jeremiah laid his complaint before God: "You are always righteous, O

LORD, when I bring a case before you. Yet I would speak with you about your justice: Why does the way of the wicked prosper? Why do all the faithless live at ease?" (Jer. 12:1).

It's a good question and one that many are still asking. In a world where 840 million people don't have enough food to eat[1] yet only 25 individuals control fortunes totaling more than $470 billion,[2] we may well ask why the rich always seem to get richer while the poor get poorer. In God's eyes, is it fair that 13 million children go to bed hungry every night in the wealthiest nation on earth?[3]

Habakkuk, another of God's prophets, challenged his boss with a similar question: "Why do you tolerate wrong?" . . . "The wicked hem in the righteous, so that justice is perverted" (Hab. 1:3-4). If Habakkuk were alive today, he might put the following questions before God:

- Why do you allow 1,300 children to be murdered or die of neglect every year in the United States?[4]
- Don't you care that 14 million children worldwide have been orphaned by AIDS?[5]
- Were you asleep when more than 150 million people were killed by war in the twentieth century?
- Doesn't it bother you that nearly half the people who commit murder get away with it?[6]

It's impossible to ignore the fact of injustice. Innocent people suffer, and God is responsible. If that bothers you, you're not alone.

Yet if Boss Spearman's notion of God was half right, it was also half wrong. We rightly conclude that God bears ultimate responsibility for what happens in the world. But we're wrong in concluding that God is unfair, for when all the evidence is heard, no jury in the world would convict God of injustice. Instead, they would perhaps marvel at two of his most important attributes: his nearly infinite patience and his unwavering sense of equality.

INFINITE PATIENCE

One day some self-righteous people, hoping to embarrass Jesus with a difficult question, hauled before him a woman who had been caught in the act of adultery (see John 7:53—8:11). Half-dressed, perhaps, and obviously guilty, the woman could have been convicted of a capital crime. By law, she might have been stoned to death.

"What's your opinion?" the smug religious teachers asked Jesus. It was a Catch-22. If Jesus affirmed that the woman should be executed, he would appear to be a hard-liner, harsh and unforgiving. If he said otherwise, he would appear soft on immorality.

Jesus didn't respond. Instead, he stooped down and began to write in the sand with his finger. But the religious big shots kept badgering him: "How about it, Rabbi? What should we do with her?"

Finally, Jesus stood. Looking directly at them, he uttered the formula that has pierced our inflated sense of self-righteousness for almost 2,000 years. "If any one of you is without sin," he said, "let him be the first to throw a stone at her" (John 8:7). Then he stooped down again and continued writing.

One by one, the hypocrites walked away, the older ones first. Why? Because they remembered at last what we would all just as soon forget: when it comes to God's law, we're all guilty, and we all deserve to die.

A False Premise

The basis of our complaint against God, as with Jeremiah's and Habakkuk's, is that suffering is unfair because we have done nothing to deserve it. We're innocent. We've been wronged. It's just not right.

That's nonsense, of course.

David, the poet-king of ancient Israel, summarized the human condition when he said, "Surely I was sinful at birth, sinful from the time my mother conceived me" (Ps. 51:5). We've all done wrong. As the apostle Paul kindly points out, "All have sinned and fall short of the glory of God" (Rom. 3:23). What's more, we know it. The little bird that sits on my shoulder and yours reminds us continually that we have done wrong. Murder? Rape? Child abuse? Perhaps not. But lying, stealing, and lust are also violations of God's law. Is there anyone who will plead "not guilty" to *all* the Ten Commandments?

And since the subject is justice, we should point out that there's only one penalty for violating God's righteous commands: death. That was God's law from the beginning, in the Garden of Eden (see Gen. 2:17), and it's still his law today (see Rom. 6:23). Every one of us has sinned, and every one of us deserves to die.

So when it comes to the issue of suffering, the real question is not *Why do we suffer unfairly?* but *Why are we still alive?* If everyone deserves the punishment of death, then in one sense no one suffers unjustly. We all deserve whatever we get—and more. By God's law, we merit something worse than cancer or blindness or persecution. We deserve to have our lives taken from us. If that's true, then every day we live is a bonus, every breath a gift. And if we suffer in the meantime, we suffer on earth at least, where there's life and love and hope, and not in hell, where there's only suffering.

So, then, why *are* we still alive?

Guided by Love

Jesus told many stories. But one stands above them all. It's his signature story, his masterpiece. It's the story about a rebellious son and a patient father. We know it as the story of the prodigal son (see Luke 15:11–32).

As the story goes, there was a young man, who when he came of age, demanded that his father give him his inheritance immediately. Rather than invest the money, further his education, or start a business, the son left home and wasted himself and his fortune on wild living. We're talking about the high life: wild parties, women, alcohol, gambling—you name it.

Meanwhile, the father waited patiently at home, hoping every day that his son would return. He had no illusions about where his son was or what he was doing. But he loved his boy, and he wanted him back, no matter what.

Finally the party ended. The money ran out, and with it the friends, the women, and the wine. The boy was destitute. "Hard times" doesn't begin to describe his existence. He lived in a pigsty, eating only what the hogs ate. He was miserable.

You know what happened next. At last the boy came to his senses and returned home, humbled and contrite. He wept before his father, begging forgiveness and asking to return only as a servant.

But the father would hear none of it. "My boy!" he cried. "My boy is home at last!"

There was a party that night, like nothing you've ever seen. The whole town was invited. There was food and wine and music and dancing. And there was the proud father, parading his son around like an astronaut just returned from the moon. And everyone who walked in the door was treated to the same speech. "This is my son," he would say. "I love him so much. I'm so proud of him."

Here's the point.

The father in that story is God. And the boy is you. And the reason you and I and every other father's son are not dead right now—as we deserve to be—is the same reason a father would watch the road every day, hoping to see his prodigal son return. It's because God loves us so much that he refused to let us go. He always holds out hope that we'll return to him and be forgiven. In spite of the fact that we deserve death, he wants to give us life. When will God finally enforce the death sentence that he has placed on the world? The apostle Peter answers that exact questions this way:

Do not forget this one thing, dear friends: With the Lord a day is like a thousand years, and a thousand years are like a day. The Lord is not slow in keeping his promise, as some understand slowness. He is patient with you, not wanting anyone to perish, but everyone to come to repentance (2 Pet. 3:8–9).

God's righteous law is that everyone who sins deserves death, and everyone has sinned. We deserve God's judgment, and we know it. Thankfully, he has extended his mercy and delayed his judgment in order to redeem us. It's an act of his grace that we live and breathe.

Still, the question remains: why do some people suffer more than others? If God is truly fair, then why does he single out some people for cancer or starvation or AIDS?

The answer is simple. He doesn't.

UNWAVERING EQUALITY

"I just don't know what I've done, Pastor." The woman shook her head mournfully, then continued in a whiney drawl. "I don't think I'm a bad person, but God must really be angry with me."

She explained. Her toaster had broken that morning. Then her refrigerator had quit, requiring a service call for repair. And the car—it wouldn't run right. Three times she had had it into the garage, yet it stalled at every stoplight.

"I know God's trying to tell me something," she whimpered. "Otherwise he wouldn't be sending all these troubles my way."

That unfortunate woman voiced a view of God held by many, a view advanced even by some theologians, that God spends most of his time practicing behavior modification on human beings. She saw herself as a voodoo doll with God holding the pins. If she were good, God would reward her with a parking spot or a check in the mail. If she behaved badly,

God would punish her by wrecking her toaster. According to her theology, every instance of suffering is the direct result of specific wrongdoing. God punishes sin, she thought, by putting a hex on the sinner.

There's just one problem with that philosophy: it's false. We know that because Jesus said so.

A Broken World

It's true that all suffering is the result of sin and is therefore God's punishment. We live in a fallen world. We live under a curse. That curse is found in Gen. 3. It stipulates, among other things, that we'll have to toil for our daily bread and that women will suffer pain in childbearing. In other words, life is hard. Yet that's true for everyone. All people have sinned, and all live under God's curse.

It's true also that the law of cause and effect applies to nearly everything in life. There are consequences for almost all behaviors, and some carry very severe natural consequences. People who smoke cigarettes place themselves at a much higher risk of developing cancer or emphysema than people who don't. People who engage in promiscuous sex are far more likely to acquire AIDS or herpes than people who don't. Life is a dangerous thing, and that's true for everyone.

Can we conclude from those facts that God punishes individual sins with specific instances of suffering? Jesus' disciples wondered the same thing (see John 9:1–5). One day when they encountered a man who had been born blind, Jesus' disciples asked, "Rabbi, who sinned, this man or his parents, that he was born blind?"

Notice that the disciples assumed that God inflicts specific suffering on people as direct punishment for individual sins. What they wondered is how long the voodoo is in effect. Might God have blinded this man for something his parents did? Jesus' answer makes short work of that notion: "Neither. . . . This happened so that the work of God might be displayed in his life" (John 9:3). Then Jesus healed the man.

Foreshadowing Peter's statement about God's patience and grace, Jesus saw the fact of suffering as an opportunity for God to redeem a broken life, not as the punishment for an individual sin. Let's make it plain: God doesn't put the whammy on people. Bad things happen to you, to me, to everybody. That's because we live in a broken world. And that makes us broken people. And God is in the business of healing broken people, not needling them. He loves us so much that he sacrificed his only son to give us eternal life (see John 3:16).

Random Evil

There's an old joke about a man who believed in determinism. By his reasoning, God specifically planned every event in his life. So when he fell down the stairs one day, he got up and said, "Whew! I'm glad *that's* over." But the Bible reveals a different picture of God, one that looks less like a puppet master and more like a parent.

Jesus said that one part of God's perfect character is that he does not play favorites. He treats all people equally. Specifically, Jesus said that God "causes his sun to rise on the evil and the good, and sends rain on the righteous and the unrighteous" (Matt. 5:45). In other words, God doesn't alter the laws of nature either to reward those who love him or to punish those who don't. If it rains, it rains on everybody. And when there are tornadoes, earthquakes, diseases, or broken toasters, they're just as likely to happen to those who "deserve" it as to those who don't. We live in a fallen world, but it's the same world for everyone. God does not single out people for suffering.

But what about Job?

When Satan asked to inflict suffering on Job, in spite of the fact that he was a righteous man, God allowed it (see Job 1:12). Yet God neither initiated Job's suffering nor prescribed it. He allowed it. That's a small point, but a telling one. As a parent, I permit my daughter to engage in behavior that puts her at risk of suffering. I allow her, for example, to ride her bike on the gravel driveway. I understand that she's likely—in fact, certain—to fall at some time. When she does, she'll feel pain. She could bleed, even break a bone. Yet I allow it. That makes me responsible for the fact that she suffers. I'm the parent, after all.

But would I *desire* for my daughter to suffer? Would I reach out to push her off the bike, ensuring that she will be hurt? What parent would? I allow her to experience pain, but I don't wish it.

Since the story of Job is given as a model, we must conclude that God treats you and me in the same way. He permits us to suffer war, natural disaster, accidents, disease, and famine, which makes him in some sense responsible. He could have prevented it but chose not to. Yet as with Job, God does not specifically inflict those evils upon individuals. Bad things happen. So do good things. And the mark of God's unwavering fairness is that he allows both good and bad things to happen to everyone.

THE VERDICT

The statement that no jury in the world would convict God of injustice is not entirely accurate. In fact, we have a precedent to the contrary. God was indicted for injustice at Auschwitz and stood trial there. He was convicted. Holocaust survivor Elie Wiesel witnessed the event as a 15-year-old and later wrote about it in his play *The Trial of God*.

Auschwitz was a Nazi death camp. Wiesel was interned there during World War II and was befriended in the camp by an older man, a Talmud scholar. Together, they studied their religion as an act of religious defiance. One night the teacher took Wiesel into a barracks where Wiesel was the only witness to a surreal court proceeding. Three masters of the Jewish law, unable to reconcile the nature of God with the hellish torture that they were living, determined to put God on trial. Robert McAfee Brown describes what happened:

> The trial lasted several nights. Witnesses were heard, evidence was gathered, conclusions were drawn, all of which issued finally in a unanimous verdict: the Lord God Almighty, Creator of Heaven and earth, was found guilty of crimes against creation and humankind. And then, after what Wiesel describes as an "infinity of silence," the Talmudic scholar looked at the sky and said "It's time for evening prayers," and the members of the tribunal recited Maariv, the evening service.[7]

That heartrending moment is a portrait of faith. We who believe in God cannot absolve him of his role in our pain. We know that he's responsible for all we experience, even suffering. He must be responsible. Who else is there?

Yet God must be worshiped. A life of unspeakable suffering may be unbearable, but a God who is not worthy of our respect, our worship, and our love would be unacceptable.

Like Jeremiah and Habakkuk and Job, like the writers of the Psalms, like the venerable Talmud scholars of Auschwitz, like people of faith in all generations, we may rail against suffering. We may vent our anger. We may question God, even accuse him. But at the end of the day, like faithful men and women in all generations, we also fall to the ground and worship him (see Job 1:12; 2:6).

After all, who else is there?

QUESTIONS FOR REFLECTION

1. Why do you think injustices like child abuse, government corruption, and terrorism arouse such strong emotions? From where do we get our sense of justice?

2. If God treated you exactly as you deserve to be treated,

what would the result be? Do you think it would be the same for other people, or different?

3. Do you prefer to think that God consciously inflicts all suffering, including minor things like stubbed toes and headaches, or that he allows us to experience the ups and downs of life in a more random fashion? Why do you feel as you do?

4. If you could ask God one question about his character, what would it be? How do you think he would respond?

5

THE DOWNSIDE UP
LEARNING TO
EMBRACE PAIN

Why did this have to happen to me?

With a sorrowful heart, I honor this pain,
And offer these tears to the rain.
—Susan Ashton, "Stand"

"Let's use the cane."

"No. I'll set it aside."

"I think it would add to the picture. It makes you look distinguished."

"The gray hair does enough of that. Besides, I can't stand this thing."

"I don't see why. It's a part of you—your persona. It makes you look . . . real."

But I hadn't come to a professional photographer in order to look real. I wanted to look *better* than real. For one moment, I wanted to stand without the use of a stick, to appear healthy and vibrant and fully alive, then to capture that moment on film and preserve it forever. How could I make this woman understand that I hated my cane and that I had no desire to use it as a prop to enhance my appearance?

I've used a walking stick off and on for some 20 years because of a disease called arthritis. Sometimes I've used crutches, at other times a wheelchair. These devices have enabled me

71

to hobble back and forth to work, to gain passage through airports, to continue functioning when my illness tried to render me immobile.

But I hate them.

I hate their appearance. I hate their foreign feel against my body. I hate being dependent on them for movement. Most of all, I hate the reminder that I'm different from other people. These devices tell me that I live with pain, that I can't control my own life, that I'm weak. I would no sooner be photographed with a cane than with a bucket of worms or a bag of garbage.

The photographer finally relented and did exactly what she had been paid to do. She created an image that shows none of my flaws, accentuates my better features, and makes me look better than I really am.

"Perfect," I said.

But was it? A perfect portrait is by definition imperfect, for no real human being is without flaws. And no one can be fully alive, fully human—perfect—who does not feel pain.

Jesus knew that, which is why he did not shrink from pain or avoid suffering; he embraced them. And that's why all the best pictures of him show his scars.

THE WORLD UPSIDE DOWN

Our culture worships beauty. Like Narcissus of Greek legend, we have become obsessed with our own image and the desire to perfect it. In the quest to improve the human body, 287,930 women in North America had liposuction procedures in 1993. More than 254,000 women had breast augmentations. In the same year, 129,774 men had their noses reshaped, and 27,985 had hair transplanted onto their balding heads.[1] We're desperate for perfection, or at least the appearance of it, so desperate that we'll undergo more than 9.6 million cosmetic procedures in any given year.[2]

Why? Why are we embarrassed by the way we look? Why

do the flaws in our bodies concern us so? We must sense that these imperfections, however slight, are evidence of our true condition. Our big noses and protruding teeth and sagging bellies, like my cane, are reminders of the fact that we're broken people. We were damaged by the Fall. We are destined to live brief lives, filled with pain. We long to be perfect, immortal. Yet even our own bodies betray us. They bear witness to the fact that we are made from dust and will return to it. We ignore this evidence if at all possible, covering it with cosmetics if we can and surgically removing it if we can't. We hide our scars. That's natural, meaning that most people do it.

But Jesus didn't. Far from being embarrassed by the human condition, he embraced it. By doing so, he not only set an example for us in how to live but also did what no cosmetologist or plastic surgeon can do: he transformed the scar into a thing of beauty.

The Great Inversion

The most generous way of describing Jesus Christ, the man, is to say that he was different. He didn't think like a normal person, and he didn't act like one. Russian novelist Feodor Dostoyevsky went further, comparing Christ to a mildly deranged prince in his novel *The Idiot.* Irreverent? Perhaps. But even a glance at the life and teaching of Jesus Christ reveals a worldview so different from our own that it seems odd, even insane, by "normal" standards. What people normally value, Jesus didn't. What they normally avoid, he embraced. The direction of his entire life is so contrary to accepted wisdom that it cannot be considered sane by any standard we know.

In his Sermon on the Mount, that masterpiece of divine wisdom, Jesus stands on its head every attitude and reaction that comes naturally to a human being. When we're injured, we seek revenge, but Jesus says to forgive losses and even be generous with those who have wronged us (see Matt. 5:39).

When people hate us, we hate them in return, but Jesus teaches us to love our enemies (see Matt. 5:44). There's more. Don't worry about the future, he advises (see Matt. 6:25), never take credit for the good you do (see Matt. 6:1), place no value in money (see Matt. 6:19), and respect others so much that you don't even think ill of them (see Matt. 7:1).

Who lives that way? No one does by his or her own nature. It's not normal. It doesn't feel right.

But it *is* right, and somewhere deep inside we know that. Maybe that's why people loved Jesus as they did and flocked to him in spite of the fact that he was not physically attractive.[3] There was something authentic about him, and he seemed perhaps more alive than anyone they had ever met. Jesus lived life upside down, and people found that life appealing in spite of themselves. They still do.

Yet all those little anomalies revealed by Jesus' teaching, those little differences between the way he thinks and the way we think, are clues to an even greater one, the grand inversion of the entire universe. For Jesus Christ did something that no Hollywood star or fashion model would consider: he gave up perfection. Jesus Christ had what each of us dreams of—a perfect form, a perfect home, a perfect life; freedom from pain, freedom from suffering, freedom from death. And he left it. He willingly took on the human form that we find so embarrassing. He chose to accept the limitations, imperfections, and pain that we try so hard to escape. He chose to suffer. He chose to die. The apostle Paul describes this incredible choice in one of the Church's earliest hymns:

[Jesus Christ], being in very nature God, did not consider equality with God something to be grasped, but made himself nothing, taking the very nature of a servant, being made in human likeness. And being found in appearance as a man, he humbled himself and became obedient to death—even death on a cross! (Phil. 2:6–8).

Consider what Paul says. Jesus Christ was God, perfect in every way, living in the splendor of heaven, having all that we long for. Yet he gave it up. He compressed himself into a tiny human shape precisely so that he would feel the limitations, pain, and frustration that we endure. Preacher and poet John Donne waxed eloquent at the thought in his muse on the birth of Christ:

> Immensity cloistered in thy dear womb,
> Now leaves his well-beloved imprisonment,
> There he has made himself to his intent
> Weak enough, now into our world to come.[4]

Ponder those words. When Christ was born, it was after nine months of captivity inside the body of a woman. The one who made all space willingly contained himself within the space of a human womb. The one who holds all power confined himself to the form of an infant. He whose voice set stars in place and planets in motion came squealing, squirming, screaming into this world as a helpless child, a child who would grow and be tempted and betrayed and beaten, a child who would feel pain, would suffer, and would die.

Why?

The Choice for Pain

The Book of Hebrews contains the grandest, most eloquent writing in the New Testament. It's perhaps the most overlooked book in Scripture. In it, an unknown writer, inspired of God, gives us the answer to this very question: Why did Jesus choose to suffer? He did so in order to become like us. And that was necessary if he were to help us. The writer of Hebrews weaves this logic throughout the opening chapters of the work, culminating in this grand statement, the spiritual touchstone of all who suffer:

> During the days of Jesus' life on earth, he offered up prayers and petitions with loud cries and tears to the one

who could save him from death, and he was heard because of his reverent submission. Although he was a son, he learned obedience from what he suffered and, once made perfect, he became the source of eternal salvation for all who obey him and was designated by God to be high priest in the order of Melchizedek (Heb. 5:7–10).

Jesus was God's son, living in the splendor and perfection of heaven. Yet in order to redeem us, in order to make the sacrifice that would finally destroy our sin and its effect, he had to become one of us. And in order to become fully human, he had to experience all that we experience. He had to be tempted, tried, and tortured. He had to suffer.

Many of us would cringe at the statement that Jesus was not perfect in heaven, yet the Bible makes it. Of course, in the way that we most often use the word "perfect," he was. He was flawless. He was perfect as a gymnast or diver who scores a 10 is perfect—he was faultless. He was without blemish, without sin. Yet the word "perfect" has a second meaning. To be perfect is to be complete, lacking nothing. And as a sacrifice for human sin, Jesus Christ was not complete, for by God's decree there could be no forgiveness of sin without the shedding of blood (see Heb. 9:22). In order to rescue us from our own sin, Jesus had to become human, had to suffer, had to die. He was made perfect, made complete as our savior, by what he suffered.

There's more at stake than our headaches and divorces and disappointments, more even than our own lives. Jesus Christ intends to remove both the suffering that we experience and the sin that caused it. His grand plan is that someday all nature will be forgiven and made new, including you and me. But in order to accomplish that, he had to die. And he chose to do so—willingly, freely, without reservation. He chose the pain.

There's more.

Follow the logic of Jesus' choice to its bitter end, and you'll arrive at the same conclusion as the apostle Paul: "Your attitude should be the same as that of Jesus Christ," he said, "who . . . did not consider equality with God something to be grasped, but made himself nothing . . . and became obedient to death" (Phil. 2:5–8). Jesus chose to suffer to provide our redemption from sin. That means we must change the way we think about pain, especially our own. That Jesus suffered in order to become like us means that when we suffer, we become like him. He embraced pain.

Can we do the same?

STANDING PAIN ON ITS HEAD

John F. Kennedy was the 35th president of the United States and was the youngest man ever to hold that office. He was handsome, athletic, virile. He was also chronically ill. Kennedy suffered from Addison's disease, a progressive illness caused by atrophy of the adrenal gland. Symptoms include increasing weakness, abnormal pigmentation of the skin and mucous membranes, weight loss, low blood pressure, and dehydration. The treatment for Addison's disease in Kennedy's day was a daily injection of cortisone, which he received. JFK also suffered from a degenerative back problem. The result was that he secretly lived in constant pain.

Yet he, like so many great men and women, did not rebel against his suffering. He apparently came to accept his condition. About his attitude toward pain, one aide remarked, "Pain was like a friend to him—it never left him, it was with him all the time." Pain became a part of Kennedy's life, a part of his identity, an experience that completed him, like a friend.

Is that possible?

It must be. What else can the apostle Paul mean by the following statement? "I want to know Christ and the power of his resurrection and the fellowship of sharing in his sufferings, becoming like him in his death" (Phil. 3:10). What else can the apostle James mean by writing, "Consider it pure joy, my brothers, whenever you face trials of many kinds" (James 1:2)? Why else would Paul flatly assert, "Your attitude should be the same as that of Christ Jesus," who chose to embrace suffering (Phil. 2:5)?

The experience of pain is always unpleasant, never to be sought. But it's not to be universally avoided or entirely rejected. God became like us by suffering. We become like him in that same way. Like Jesus, we become more real, more perfect, when we feel pain.

To Embrace Pain Is More Authentic

There's an old gag about a middle-aged woman who was promised by God that she would live to be 80 years old. "Since I'll be around for 30 more years," she reasoned, "I might as well get some work done." So she went to a plastic surgeon and asked for the works. The doctor performed every imaginable cosmetic procedure, and the results were amazing. The woman became a stunning beauty. Two days later, she stepped off the curb and was hit by a bus. She died instantly. Arriving in heaven, she questioned God about the incident. "I thought you said I'd live to be 80," the woman demanded. "What happened?"

"I didn't recognize you," was God's reply.

The impertinent humor hits close to home. We pander to beauty. If life were free from pain, free from unpleasantness, free from any blemish, so we think, it would be perfect. We hunger to be something we cannot be: flawless. Yet in our quest for that perfection, we become less human—even less godly—than we were before. One beautiful woman, Oscar-winning actress Halle Berry, could warn us of that trap. "Beauty?" she ponders. "Let me tell you something—being thought of as a beautiful woman has spared me nothing in life, no heartache, no trouble. . . . Beauty is essentially meaningless, and it is always transitory."[5]

Is she wrong?

When we look for a life without pain, and without reminders of pain—blemishes, imperfections, scars—we long for something false. Life simply isn't that way, no matter how flawless it may appear on the screen or in magazines or popular culture. What the plastic surgeon promises, he or she can never deliver. We're damaged. We can ignore that fact, but we can't change it.

So what does it mean to embrace pain? Is pain somehow good or desirable, something to hunger for? Should we refuse analgesics or even seek to inflict pain upon ourselves? By no means. Pain is neither good nor something to be sought. Yet it's inevitable. Therefore, we gain nothing by rebelling against it, railing at God or ourselves or others because pain exists or because we feel it.

To embrace pain is to acknowledge that we're fully human. "If you suffer," muses Elbert Hubbard, "thank God—it is a sure sign you are alive."[6] We are most human when we suffer, just as Jesus was. Embracing pain will change our attitude about ourselves. We will come to see our flawed, scarred, imperfect lives for what they are: evidence that we live in a broken world—but live nonetheless.

To embrace pain is to adopt a realistic attitude about the world and our place in it. Anger, resentment, depression—these are the fruit of rebellion against reality. When we acknowledge that to be human is to be broken, we find peace, we're able to love ourselves and live as free people.

To embrace pain is to become familiar with heroes, great men and women who have lived lives of beauty, purpose, and grand achievement in spite of what they suffered. When we accept the pain in our own lives, we have something in common with Abraham Lincoln, Helen Keller, the apostle Paul, Ann Frank, and countless others who lived grand lives in spite of grief, loneliness, disability, or persecution. To embrace pain is to grow from suffering rather than be weakened by it.

To embrace pain is to be real, to be authentic, to be human. It is to live our lives without embarrassment but with confidence, without despair but with purpose, without resentment over what we endure but with joy at the fact that we live at all. To embrace pain is to embrace life, and there's only one alternative.

To embrace pain is to accept our limitations while relying on God for strength, which is nothing less than Jesus did. When he prayed in the Garden, he cried for release from suffering yet accepted his path with the words "Your will be done."

To embrace pain is to accept the scars—physical, emotional, spiritual—that are left upon our souls and to see them for what they truly are—reminders of the fact that human life, if anything, is painful and that those who will be redeemed must first be broken.

To embrace pain is to be honest. To embrace pain is to be real.

It Is More Christlike

Pain is what makes us fully human, as Jesus knew. And to accept pain makes us more like Christ, as Paul discovered. For we become like him when we suffer, or rather when we adopt his attitude toward suffering. Jesus chose to suffer; he chose to die. It is true that he felt anxiety about death. "My Father, if it is possible," he prayed in the Garden, "may this cup be taken from me" (Matt. 26:39). Those words, so honest, so human, show that he did not relish pain any more than we do. Yet he accepted it. "Yet not as I will, but as you will." He knew that pain was as necessary for his mission as was life. He had to suffer, and in the end he chose to. We become like Christ when we recognize the inevitability of pain and accept it, when we embrace not the hurt but the good that can come in no way except through it.

To burn the selfishness out of me is a painful thing. It's by disappointment and failure and by feeling the bitter sting of remorse that I see myself finally, fully, for the sinful man that I am apart from him. To expose that selfishness brings a pain sharper than the surgeon's knife. But that pain is a needed thing. For only when sin is exposed can the healing salve of God's grace be applied. We cannot receive mercy without first feeling the pain of brokenness, shame, guilt.

To live every day with a chronic illness is frustrating, depressing, infuriating. Yet when I feel pain in my legs, I remember that I am dust and that I must rely on the Creator for all things. It's pain that causes me to embrace the blessed words of Christ "Even the very hairs of your head are all numbered. So don't be afraid" (Matt. 10:30–31). Pleasure can never drive me to rely upon him.

To lose a beloved member of my family—my own child— caused pain I have no wish to describe. Yet in that experience I saw the grief of God over my own sin and the death of his son that was the inevitable result. Others might have understood the love of God apart from sorrow. I never did. My heart was molded to his by that pain.

When we seek at all costs to avoid pain, suffering, and ugliness, we deny the reality of our own humanity and our need for redemption, and we are as unlike Christ as we can be. The challenge of being an authentic disciple is not to become flawless, for we are flawed people. It's rather to adopt the mind of Christ in all things, that beautiful, compelling, frightening attitude that sees pain not as an enemy but a comrade, something not to be sought, neither shunned, a thing neither loved nor feared nor hated but calmly accepted.

Why me? we sometimes wonder. *Why did my life have to turn out this way?* Indeed, why not? If all people suffer, if Christ himself suffered, if we cannot become in some sense perfect without suffering, then why not me? Why not you? The centerpiece of Jesus' teaching, illustrated so perfectly by his own birth, life, and death, is that suffering is an essential part of being human. And ever since God became man, suffering is also an essential experience for becoming like God. Let this same mind be in you that was in Christ Jesus.

THE PERFECT PICTURE

I let her take the picture—finally.

I sat on the chair, there in the photographer's studio, surrounded by lights, feeling as if the whole world were watching. I leaned forward a little, resting my hands on my cane, and stared down the lens of the camera as if into the face of God.

It flashed.

The picture revealed a different me than the one before, more sober, more plain, more honest—more real. I went home that night and stood before the mirror, alone, counting the scars on my body. Six surgeries on my legs have left them riddled with ugly red lines. How I have been ashamed of them. How I have hated them. How anxiously I have hidden them from view.

No more.

I have seen the scars on Jesus' body. I have learned that all real people have scars. All survivors have scars. All heroes have scars. All who have lived and loved and bled and lost and failed and triumphed have scars. It's the plastic people who are perfect, the unreal people, the airbrushed, digitally enhanced people who can't survive outside the strange and surreal environment of a magazine page or movie frame. We who are missing a limb or walk with a limp or are married to an insulin needle or are divorced or abused or hungry or hurt—we're real.

So I embrace these scars, my stigmata, my marks of Christ. For just as he, through suffering, became like me, so I, by my pain, have become more like him. These scars have become my seminary course in Christlikeness. For by them I have learned to be honest with myself, honest with God, and totally dependent upon him.

That's not easy. Faith never is. Life never is. But Jesus did this: he embraced the pain and triumphed. He suffered, he died, he lived. He made it, and we will too.

So "let us fix our eyes on Jesus, the author and perfecter of our faith, who for the joy set before him endured the cross, scorning its shame. . . . Consider him who endured such opposition from sinful men, so that you will not grow weary and lose heart" (Heb. 12:2–3).

QUESTIONS FOR REFLECTION

1. When you feel pain or suffer in other ways, do you ever feel singled out or different from "normal" people?

2. To what lengths would you go to avoid pain or suffering of some sort?

3. Is there a difference between suffering that has a purpose and suffering that has no purpose?

4. Do you have scars on your body? How do you feel about them? Embarrassed? Indifferent? Proud? Why do you feel as you do?

6

JUST DESERTS
HOW WE BECOME
LIKE GOD

Don't I deserve better?

No pain, no palm; No thorns, no throne;
No gall, no glory; No cross, no crown.
—William Penn

The Medal of Honor is the highest award for military valor that the United States of America can bestow. Usually presented by the president in the name of Congress, it's most often called the Congressional Medal of Honor. The decoration was created in 1861 to honor sailors and marines who displayed "gallantry in action" during the Civil War. The Philadelphia Mint originally created 200 medals for the Secretary of the Navy.[1] Since the first award was presented to Private Jacob Parrott and five others on March 25, 1863, a total of 3,459 people representing every branch of the U. S. military service have been awarded the medal, including nine unknown individuals, for 3,440 acts of personal bravery. Nineteen courageous persons have received this honor twice.

The guidelines followed today for awarding the Medal of Honor are quite simple. They were established by an act of Congress on July 25, 1963. By law, the award may be given only for acts of bravery that go above and beyond the call of duty, risking one's life in the face of the enemy. No one may request this honor for himself or herself. It's bestowed by the president upon only a few who display exceptional valor without thought for their own lives.

This award is for heroes.

Heroes are those who count their lives as nothing compared to the cause, those who suffer, even die, for the sake of gain. We honor those who are willing to risk their lives or lose them. We honor brave men like Fred Renz, a Menlo Park, California, real estate executive who tells of his service as a young man in the Korean War. As a fighter pilot, he swooped into enemy territory under intense fire to save the lives of 152 Marines and soldiers. And we stand in awe of selfless heroes like retired bread truck driver Jackie Albert Stern, who was photographed at a Florida sheriff's office with the Medal of Honor resplendent on his chest; and Illinois judge Michael F. O'Brien, who let it be known that he had not one but two Medals of Honor for Navy service off the coast of Lebanon in 1958.[2]

The problem with those particular "heroes," however, is that they are frauds. Their military service is either nonexistent or exaggerated. They committed no acts of bravery, no feats of valor. Their Medals of Honor were fakes. They claimed an honor, and even wore its coveted decoration that they had never earned. This is not uncommon. Since 1954, more than 500 Medal of Honor frauds have been exposed.[3] In some cases, men claimed this prestigious honor for years, deceiving their families and friends and taking places of honor in Memorial Day parades.

Cowards. Frauds. Liars. We abhor men like that, people who claim an honor that they haven't won. They dishonor themselves and their country. Most of all, they dishonor the memory of the brave men and women, known and unknown, who gave their lives for a great cause.

Yet we are like them. We honor those who sacrifice for others, yet we're nearly always unwilling to suffer ourselves. We seek the glory of heaven yet would bypass the vale of tears. We would wear the crown of Christ without its thorns. We would accept the glory of heaven without experiencing the pain of death. We honor heroes, yet we live as cowards.

Jesus shows us a different way.

No Pain, No Gain

It's an article of faith in American culture that you really can get something for nothing. The American dream is a story of upward mobility, and it has come true before. Some struck it rich in the silver mines of Colorado. Others made a fortune in California gold or Texas oil. Steel, railroads, automobiles, microchips—certainly there must be a way for anyone to gain a fortune with little or no investment. Every day we're bombarded by direct-mail flyers, billboards, and popup ads that promise some aspect of the good life for nothing.

- Zero-percent interest or $3,000 cash back!
- No down payment and no interest for two years!
- Earn $100,000 per year in your spare time!
- Lose weight without dieting!

It's nonsense, of course. Nothing good comes without labor, risk, or sacrifice. California prospectors risked their lives for gold, and many died. The few who became rich did so with no small risk to themselves. Many immigrants to the New World have risen to great heights. Most have not. Between 1892 and 1954, approximately 12 million immigrants stepped off a boat at Ellis Island, New York.[4] Most of them arrived with nothing but the clothes on their backs. They toiled merely to survive. We live on a continent still bursting with prospect, yet since the nation's founding, 651,008 Americans have been killed in battle and another 1,431,290 wounded in order to provide that freedom and opportunity for others.[5] Nothing is gained without toil, sacrifice, or pain. It's the law of the universe that no good thing comes without effort.

And it's God's law.

We would always rather believe that God's design for the world—and especially for those of us who call ourselves his children—calls for health, wealth, and prosperity. If God loves us, we reason, he certainly wants us to be happy. And, we reason, that happiness must include good things like freedom from pain and material comfort. God will give these things to us because, well—we deserve them. God exists to bless us. We exist in order to be blessed. It's a match made in heaven.

Yet the whole of God's Word describes a different arrangement. After Adam and Eve disobeyed God, he cursed the earth. Specifically, that curse included the stipulation that we must work in order to survive. God said to Adam,

> Cursed is the ground because of you; through painful toil you will eat of it all the days of your life. It will produce thorns and thistles for you, and you will eat the plants of the field. By the sweat of your brow you will eat your food until you return to the ground (Gen. 3:17–19).

We survive by working. And work is unpleasant. That's the way the world is. Until the effects of the curse are finally removed in the end, there will be no free lunch. Toil, which is by definition painful, will be a part of human life. No pain, no gain.

That principle applies to spiritual things as well as physical ones. We do not gain spiritually, we do not grow, without labor. We do not apprehend the good things that God has in store for us without effort. That's the central lesson of the most exciting period in the history of God's people, recorded in the Book of Joshua.

When the Hebrew people were slaves in Egypt, God sent Moses to deliver them (see Exodus, especially chap. 3). God promised to lead them into a land flowing with milk and honey—in other words, a land of plenty and opportunity. What a gift! Yet as the people prepared to enter into the Promised Land, which was indeed a bountiful place, it turned out that there was one small problem: the land was inhabited by strong people living in heavily fortified cities who had no intention of allowing the Israelites to take possession of "their" land (See Num. 13, especially vv. 27–28). In order to seize God's promise, they had to fight for it. The Book of Joshua is largely a military history, recording the conquest of the land of Canaan. No pain, no gain.

It's noteworthy that even Jesus, in his ministry of compassion, nearly always called upon people to demonstrate their faith by taking some action. When he healed people, he told them variously to stand up (see Mark 3:3), show themselves to the priests (see Matt. 8:4), and stretch out their arms (see Luke 6:10). These were sick people, yet Jesus forced them to take some action in order to receive the blessing he offered. The same is true for us. As James reminds us, the perfecting of our faith—the perfecting of ourselves—requires painful trials (see James 1:1–2). God does not simply dispense love, joy, peace, patience, kindness, goodness, faithfulness, gentleness, and self-control like lollipops to children. To become patient, we must face situations that try our patience. To cultivate joy, we must face circumstances that tempt us to despair. To acquire virtue, we must struggle, wrestling, like Jacob, to take hold of God's blessing. Elisabeth Kübler-Ross wrote,

> The most beautiful people we have known are those who have known defeat, known suffering, known struggle, known loss, and have found their way out of the depths. These persons have an appreciation, a sensitivity, and an understanding of life that fills them with compassion, gentleness, and a deep loving concern. Beautiful people do not just happen.[6]

No pain, no gain. It's still true.

THE PATH TO GLORY

"We must somehow believe that unearned suffering is redemptive," said Martin Luther King Jr.[7] That's not merely the hope-filled wish of an oppressed person. Rather, it's a truth grounded in the living Word of God; for the life of Jesus Christ shows us the pathway to glory, and it leads through suffering.

Some journeys begin in an unlikely direction. In order to travel south from my home, I must first go north. The only road leads away from the goal; so I must take it first and then change direction. In order to gain wealth, one must risk loss. It takes money to make money, as the saying holds, so in order to create a successful business, one must first give money away, investing in hope of a return. And the road to glory leads also in an unlikely direction. For the path toward the things we most crave begins with a step in the opposite direction. For the way up begins by going down. If we would gain, we must first lose. And when we do, we have hope of something greater.

Jesus tried very hard to tell us that. "Whoever wants to save his life will lose it," he said, "but whoever loses his life for me and for the gospel will save it" (Mark 8:35). The lesson is that by going directly at the things we want—security, contentment, meaning—we'll miss them. Yet when we're willing to let go of our lives, embrace suffering, and even come to terms with death, we discover a much more meaningful life, a life filled with purpose. And Jesus not only taught that lesson—he also lived it. He walked that opposite path, the one that leads first away from the goal, when he left heaven to live among us. The apostle Paul traces that unlikely route for us in his letter to the Philippians:

> Your attitude should be the same as that of Christ Jesus: Who, being in very nature God, did not consider equality with God something to be grasped, but made himself nothing, taking the very nature of a servant, being made in human likeness. And being found in appearance as a man, he humbled himself and became obedient to death—even death on a cross! Therefore God exalted him to the highest place and gave him the name that is above every name, that

at the name of Jesus every knee should bow, in heaven and on earth and under the earth, and every tongue confess that Jesus Christ is Lord, to the glory of God the Father (Phil. 2:5–11).

Jesus humbled himself to accept circumstances that were beneath him, to say the very least. Unlike you and me, he had the option to avoid suffering. But he chose to embrace it in order to achieve a greater goal than even self-preservation. By choosing to suffer, he earned the salvation of the world. By doing so, he has been awarded the high place, the highest honor in all creation, and one day every created being will bow before him in reverence and awe, honoring him for the sacrifice he made on the Cross.

So it works. You really can arrive in the north by heading south. By suffering, we enter an experience that we have no wish to embrace. Pain is not our destination. Yet through it, we grow to become something we were not, something better, nobler, more virtuous. That's why the apostle James insisted, "Consider it pure joy, my brothers, whenever you face trials of many kinds, because you know that the testing of your faith develops perseverance. Perseverance must finish its work so that you may be mature and complete, not lacking anything" (James 1:2–4). The road to glory—completion, perfection—involves difficulty, pain, suffering. It's down this path we must travel if we would become truly like Christ. He walked that path ahead of us, and we must follow him.

But where does it lead, and what are the results?

Pain Improves Character

Years ago I played on a church basketball team that may have had the worst record in history. One boy on our team was dribbling the ball toward the goal when an opposing player crashed into him, stole the ball, and took off in the other direction. Everyone saw that it was a flagrant foul—everyone except the referee. There was no whistle. My father, sitting in the stands next to the father of my teammate, remarked on the unfairness of the call—or lack thereof. The boy's father was unfazed. "It's good for him," he snorted. "Builds character."

That homespun wisdom could have been lifted from the pages of Scripture, for the writer of Hebrews makes the identical point to the Christians of the first century. When you suffer, think of it as discipline—and God knows that you need discipline in order to build your character.

> Endure hardship as discipline; God is treating you as sons. For what son is not disciplined by his father? If you are not disciplined (and everyone undergoes discipline), then you are illegitimate children and not true sons. Moreover, we have all had human fathers who disciplined us and we respected them for it. How much more should we submit to the Father of our spirits and live! Our fathers disciplined us for a little while as they thought best; but God disciplines us for our good, that we may share in his holiness. No discipline seems pleasant at the time, but painful. Later on, however, it produces a harvest of righteousness and peace for those who have been trained by it (Heb. 12:7–11).

God is not in the business of inflicting suffering on people, as Job demonstrates. Yet he's quite willing to use any and everything we experience in order to refine our character. When we begin to see life's experiences, both the good and the bad, in this light, we grow. We learn patience by having our patience tried. We become kind by overcoming the temptation to selfishness. We learn forgiveness by experiencing betrayal or cruelty. No soldier has ever liked boot camp. Neither does God expect that we'll enjoy frustration, injustice, or pain. Yet by them we grow to become better, more godlike people. Discipline in the form of suffering can shape our behavior for the better.

And in some instances, what we suffer results directly from our behavior. God placed consequences for behavior into our world, and we bump against them all the time. Self-indulgence brings remorse. Sexual promiscuity may result in shame, broken relationships, even disease. The abuse of alcohol or other drugs can lead to addiction. There are lessons in the pain, not that we're always willing to learn them. Lord Conesford said cheekily, "I have every sympathy with the American who was so horrified by what he has read on the effects of smoking that he gave up reading." Many people approach the experience of suffering in that way. Rather than learn the lesson from pain, they persist in the very behaviors that lead to it. Discipline is not always effective, yet to the extent that we're willing to learn from the pain, we grow, and our lives become better.

Pain Refines Attitude

If pain can influence the way we behave, it can also affect the way we think. Jesus constantly urged his followers to place greater value on the next life than on this one, and the experience of suffering helps us do that.

They call it the thousand-yard stare. It's the glazed look and blank expression of a war-weary soldier. Veterans and journalists who have experienced war firsthand report seeing it in others, even in themselves. Having seen too much of death, brutality, and destruction, having come to believe that their own lives can be lost at any time—and probably will be—combat-fatigued soldiers begin to look beyond the scene before their eyes. Staring into space, they seem to be in touch with a different reality. They have no eyes for this world; they've seen too much of it. The experience of suffering can have a similar—and more positive—effect on a believer.

Jesus warned constantly of two dangers: self-righteousness and attachment to wealth. He was most caustic about the first and most persistent about the second. Self-important people have a hard time avoiding hell, Jesus warned (see Matt. 23:33), and rich people have a hard time getting into heaven (see Mark

10:25). The problem in both cases is overattention to self and the things that make life comfortable. It's frightfully easy to become obsessed with our own egos, success, money, and possessions. We may easily forget that there's a spiritual world and that it's where we'll spend eternity. We can become so wrapped up in the here-and-now that we lose sight of forever.

Pain fixes that.

Nothing loosens our grip on the things around us quite like suffering. Nothing opens our eyes to how weak and frail we are quite like pain. Nothing is quite as effective as failure in helping us see ourselves accurately. People who have suffered a great deal develop a thousand-yard stare of the soul. They see the present reality too well and begin to look beyond it. They become loose with the world, because they realize it's not a forever thing. Their attitudes toward themselves, success, money, and even relationships, change. They're not so afraid of death because they're not so attached to life. They're more willing to give, more willing to risk, less concerned with self, and more attentive to others. They realize that they're dust.

It's by giving our lives away that we actually keep them. Those who experience only comfort have no desire to give themselves away. They cling tightly to ego, status, money, and things. Those who have suffered have learned to let go. They rely on God in a way that was impossible before.

Pleasure is a particularly ineffective lens through which to view reality. Suffering, painful as it may be, provides a more accurate view of the world and helps us to think right about who we are and what comes next. It's suffering that prepares us for glory.

NOT MEDALS BUT SCARS

According to Title XVIII of the United States Code, it's a crime punishable by imprisonment for any person to knowingly wear the Medal of Honor who has not been awarded it.

Jackie Albert Stern was convicted of that crime and was sentenced to one year of probation in December 1996. The judge ordered him to write a letter of apology to every living recipient of the Medal of Honor and have the letter published in the newspaper on Memorial Day 1997. Fred Renz was sentenced in December 1997 after pleading guilty to unauthorized wearing of the medal. A federal magistrate in San Francisco fined him $2,500, gave him a year's probation, and ordered him into drug, alcohol, and psychiatric counseling.

The world is hard on fake heroes.

Those who would claim Christlikeness without first becoming like Christ in his suffering will fare no better in the courts of heaven. For as Elbert Hubbard has pointed out, when you get to heaven, "God will not look you over for medals, degrees, or diplomas, but for scars."[8] It's the path through suffering that leads us to glory.

For what it's worth, the last two men to receive the Medal of Honor were Gary Gordon and Randall Shughart. On October 3, 1993, in Mogadishu, Somalia, these men, members of the elite unit known as "The Delta Force," were involved in an action against Somalian warlords. Two United States helicopters, Blackhawks, were shot down. At one crash site, four injured crewmen lay helpless, surrounded by hostile forces. Knowing that their lives might be forfeited, Gordon and Shughart fought their way through a dense maze of shanties and shacks to reach and defend the critically injured crewmen. The two patrolled the perimeter, defending their comrades against withering fire.

After his teammate was fatally wounded and his own rifle ammunition exhausted, Gordon returned to the wreckage, recovered a rifle with five rounds of ammunition remaining, and gave it to the downed helicopter pilot with the words "Good luck." Armed only with a pistol, Gordon continued to fight until he was fatally wounded. His actions saved the pilot's life.

On May 23, 1994, in a small ceremony in the East Room of the White House, President Bill Clinton presented the posthumous award to the widows of those two brave men. The citation for their award states, "Master Sergeant Gordon's extraordinary heroism and devotion to duty were in keeping with the highest standards of military service and reflect great credit upon him, his unit and the United States Army."[9]

Those actions also are a reminder of that truth, so evident in Scripture, so eloquently displayed in the life of Christ, that the path to glory can lead only through sacrifice. For when we seek only our own comfort, we achieve no noble thing and can never become like the Master. It's when we embrace trials, accept pain, and spend our lives for others that we become like him in his glory.

QUESTIONS FOR REFLECTION

1. Do you think it's a fair assessment to say that we often look for the easy way out of difficult circumstances? Explain your answer.

2. Can you think of some occasions in which your behavior has been shaped by painful experiences?

3. How has the experience of suffering affected the value you place on things like money, possessions, and relationships?

4. Are you afraid to die?

7

THE NEEDLE AND THE THORN
GOD'S ANSWER TO PAIN

Why won't God heal me?

Who best bear his mild yoke, they serve him best. . . .
They also serve who only stand and wait.
—John Milton, "Sonnet: On His Blindness"

The surgery was fine. The recovery was horrible. Even that wasn't too bad until they took away the morphine.

It was noon on August 26, 1992, and I had undergone knee-replacement surgery only a couple of hours earlier. Armed with tools similar to those found in a junior high shop class, a pair of surgeons had sliced open my leg, sawn off the ends of my femur and tibia, and screwed into place a metal-and-plastic contraption shaped exactly like a human knee joint. They closed the hole with staples.

So far, so good. I survived the operation—always a delightful surprise—and was transported to a hospital room where I sat up in bed, chatting with my father and eating Jell-O. "Nice day," I commented. The regional anesthesia that blocked all sensation below my navel was still in effect, and I felt fine. But as the anesthetic began to wear off, I felt pain in my leg. It was mild at first, like a headache, then more intense, like a crushing weight. I told the nurse. "No problem," she replied cheerfully,

"We'll get you some nice pain medicine." With that, she activated a device that delivered small doses of morphine directly into my bloodstream.

But there was a problem. My body reacted badly to the drug. Rather than risk serious complications, my physician made the choice to discontinue the administration of analgesics. They took away the drugs. For five hours I endured the aftermath of joint replacement surgery without the benefit of narcotics. Worse, nurses, doctors, family members, friends, chaplains, and even total strangers tried to relieve the pain by other means.

"You're doing great," they said.

"Take some deep breaths."

"Try to relax."

"We're praying for you."

"Let's try some ice."

"Maybe if you didn't scream so much . . ."

Nothing worked. What I needed was a narcotic. What I got was a pat on the back and lots of advice. So I suffered, not very patiently. And between the stabs of pain and white-knuckled pleas for a needle, this thought darted in and out of my mind: *Why is this happening to me? If God really can heal people, then why doesn't he heal me—right now?*

To anyone who is now suffering, any answer to that question will seem like so much attaboy and ice. In the presence of acute pain, life-threatening illness, or chronic disease, a discourse of the nature of God is more useless than ticks on a dog. Rather than providing comfort, such words may actually inflame anger and intensify the pain. People who suffer have a single focus: finding relief.

Yet there's only one source for relief from pain. It comes always from God. For it's God who relieves suffering, God who provides the grace to bear it, and God who will finally abolish it completely.

GOD RELIEVES PAIN

When we suffer, we want relief. "Make the pain stop" may be the most common words spoken by anyone who suffers. The more than four billion dollars spent each year on pain relievers for headaches and other pain testifies to our desire for comfort.[1] We don't tolerate pain well. God knows that, which is why he so often alleviates suffering in a direct way by removing it.

When Jesus walked the earth, he was known as a healer. Very early in his public ministry, Jesus visited the home of Simon (whom Jesus called Peter) in Capernaum. Simon's mother-in-law was in bed with a fever, and Jesus heard about it. He took her by the hand, helped her out of bed, and the fever left her. She was healed. The news spread quickly, and that evening a horde of people crowded around the door of Simon's home; Jesus healed them (see Mark 1:29–34). That event marked the beginning of a period of intense miraculous activity in Jesus' ministry. He healed the sick, cast out demons, caused blind people to see, multiplied food, and even stilled a violent storm. The things we fear most—disease, disability, hunger, catastrophe—Jesus eliminated. Where people suffered, Jesus put an end to their suffering.

Does God still do that?

Miraculous Healing

In September 1987 my brother, a college sophomore, began feeling ill. He visited the university health office, where the school nurse suspected mononucleosis, common enough among 19-year-olds. She sent him to see a doctor. The physician also figured Jonathan's flu-like symptoms to be a case of mono, which can drag on for several weeks. So no one was surprised when Joe, as we call him, was still under the weather when he attended a Halloween party at my sister's home.

"I don't like the look of that swelling in your neck," my sister said as he arrived. The enlarged area below my brother's ear was clearly visible in spite of the upturned collar on his jacket. She called the doctor immediately, and he examined Joe that evening. The next day the physician performed a biopsy on the swollen tissue, "just to be on the safe side." Everyone knew he suspected cancer. The tissue was analyzed at the local hospital, and samples were sent to the Mayo Clinic to confirm the diagnosis. The process took several days.

In the meantime, we prayed for Joe, asking God to heal him.

About two weeks later, my father was summoned to the doctor's office to hear the test results. "It's not good," the doctor began gravely. "Your son has malignant lymphoma of a very aggressive type. We need to begin chemotherapy immediately. The test results indicate that his liver may already be involved, perhaps other organs as well."

The doctor had just pronounced a death sentence upon my brother.

"But he's better," my father protested.

"What do you mean he's 'better'?"

"I mean he looks better, his appetite has returned, the swelling has gone down in his neck. He's better."

"That's impossible," the physician said flatly. "That can't happen without treatment. Not with this disease."

But it *did* happen. We prayed for my brother to be well, and he was well. The next day a doctor's exam confirmed my father's report. The incredulous physician called the Mayo Clinic and suggested that the diagnosis was incorrect. But there had been no error in the analysis. My brother was miraculously healed, and his symptoms never returned. To this day, my father carries the lab report from the hospital in his Bible as a reminder of the fact that God still heals.

There are hundreds of occasions of divine healing recorded in Scripture, and nearly everyone can name some instance of healing or relief of suffering that cannot be explained as having happened by ordinary means. Over and over, Scripture describes God as "compassionate and gracious" (See Exod. 34:6; 2 Chron. 30:9; Neh. 9:17; among many other scriptures).

Why doesn't God do something about suffering? Very often he does. God witnesses suffering, and it moves him to action. He takes pity on those who feel pain, and he heals.

If that's true, then why doesn't God relieve *all* suffering? Why doesn't he heal *everyone,* take away *all* pain, empty *every* hospital, dry *every* tear? Why does God ignore the suffering of so many people and do nothing?

Is that really the case?

"Natural" Healing

Healing, in the broadest sense, is God's primary objective in the world. He aims to heal, or restore, the world that was damaged by the Fall, and he does that all the time. He heals constantly. In fact, every instance of healing must be attributed to God.

When the human body is injured, it will attempt to heal itself. Flesh closes on its own after being cut. Bones that have been broken mend themselves. The body attempts to purge toxins from itself. "The body heals itself; the physician is only nature's assistant" is a saying often attributed to Hippocrates, the father of medicine. Benjamin Franklin was less polite, saying, "Nature performs the cure, but the physician takes the fee." God created us in such a way that our bodies can restore themselves. That they're unable to do so completely is the result of the Fall; our mortal bodies are bound for decay, for we were taken from the ground and will return to it (see Gen. 3:19). Yet this "natural" healing is an act of God's grace. Scabs and scars are really evidence of the truth that God is in the business of salvaging damaged goods. He fixes things.

Medical Healing

Thirteen-month-old Connor Jones is as cute as a button.

Without a close examination, you would never know that there had ever been anything wrong with him. But Connor is a little thick around the middle, and it's not just baby fat. As a pre-born child, Connor suffered from a condition called "prune belly syndrome," which is caused by an obstruction of the bladder. The condition was detected during an ultrasound halfway through his mother's pregnancy. The swelling caused by Connor's obstruction could have caused his bladder to rupture or his lungs to be crushed. Most children who suffer from this syndrome die within minutes of birth. Yet Connor is alive and well.

Before Connor was born, Michael Gravett twice performed delicate prenatal surgery, poking a needle through the belly of Sarah Jones to get to her unborn child and drain his distended bladder. Those surgical procedures, performed before Connor's birth, saved his life.[2]

Prenatal surgery is an instance of what some would call a medical miracle. Physicians, armed with knowledge and skill far beyond what any of us are born with, are able to operate on preborn children, replace diseased joints, transplant human organs, graft skin, regulate blood sugar, clear clogged arteries, and perform countless other procedures that heal disease, restore broken bodies, and relieve suffering.

Fish can't do that. Neither can dogs, gorillas, or horses. Yet human beings can apply knowledge and skill to the art of healing and, in many cases, relieve suffering in ways that seem just as miraculous today as did Jesus' healings in the first century. Why? Because God has given us a certain mastery over the world and its natural processes. We were charged at Creation to "fill the earth and subdue it" (Gen. 1:28), and we retain that dominion in spite of our fallen condition. We have the power to heal, in a limited way, because God gave it to us. In that sense, Franklin's observation rings even more true. God gives the skill, and the physician collects the fee. All healing, whether miraculous, "natural," or physician induced, comes from God.

Miracles? They are, as C. S. Lewis has pointed out, merely an intense or high-speed instance of the healing that God is always doing in the world. They're a "close and small" glimpse of God's grace in action. If God did not constantly relieve suffering in the world, what would life be like? What if bleeding never stopped, if weary muscles never gained strength, if the sun never rose, if there were no springtime? We have all these things because God made them; he is the God who heals.

But what about *me?* The question of healing always becomes a personal one. Why doesn't God heal *my* illness? Why does *my* child suffer? Where's the miracle in *my* life? Why can't the doctors find a cure for *my* wife's disease? If it's true that God is a healer, it's also true that he does not heal every person, at least not in an immediate way. In spite of miracle reports, in spite of natural healing, in spite of the physician's skill, people suffer.

What about *them?*

GOD GIVES GRACE

Nobody knows what it was for certain. Some think it was epilepsy. Others believe it was a speech impediment, like stuttering. Some even surmise that the apostle Paul's famous "thorn in the flesh" was not a physical ailment at all but some form of stress or persecution. Whatever the problem was, Paul suffered greatly from it and prayed for God to remove it. Like nearly every person who has suffered from migraine headaches, arthritis, or diabetes, Paul begged God for relief. Three times the great apostle pleaded with God to take away this "thorn." Three times God said no. Paul was not healed (see 2 Cor. 12:7–9). Yet in his affliction, Paul discovered an act of God's mercy that was every bit as powerful as healing: God gave Paul the ability to endure. When Paul cried for help, God said, as Paul relates it, "My grace is sufficient for you, for my power is made perfect in weakness" (v. 9). It was through suffering that Paul came to rely fully on God. It was because of Paul's weakness that he discovered God's greater strength.

The Power of Weakness

Paul was not the first to discover the power of weakness. Moses suffered from a speech impediment. Rather than removing the problem, God provided a solution. Moses' brother, Aaron, spoke for him (see Exod. 6:30—7:2). As a result, Moses was forced to rely upon God rather than oratorical skill when confronting Pharaoh. Jacob's hip was dislocated; he walked with a limp. As a result, he was forced to remember the struggle that had finally brought him face-to-face with God. Jacob's disability became a reminder for generations of Israelites that we come close to God through our struggles (see Gen. 32:22–32).

These stories are not placed in the Bible for no reason. They are there precisely to remind us that it's through the experience of weakness—specifically suffering—that we're made to rely on God. Samson was perfectly healthy and stronger than any 10 men. Yet, his life was a series of tragedies caused by his own hubris. His strength was his greatest weakness. David was Israel's great warrior king, handsome, talented, and highly skilled. His reign was marked by tragedy, beginning with his affair with Bathsheba and subsequent murder of her husband Uriah. David's success caused him to rely on himself, not God. Moses, Jacob, Paul—these men were broken, and that brokenness led them eventually to cast themselves entirely into God's hands. When God does not heal us, he draws us close. When we feel pain, we may be closer to God than at any other time in our lives.

Eyes on the Prize

All who suffer have this in common: we want to know that our suffering serves some purpose. We look for some good, if not in the pain itself then at least in us. The God who redeems all things redeems pain as well, for God works in us even—and perhaps especially—when we suffer. We gain power in suffering by relying more fully on God. We also gain clarity by being reminded of what matters most.

The apostle Paul, whose thorn in the flesh caused him so much anxiety, suffered many things in life. He was shipwrecked, beaten, slandered, stoned, and falsely imprisoned. Yet he endured these things calmly, even cheerfully, because he knew that his life was fixed on a goal. Paul puts it this way:

> Therefore we do not lose heart. Though outwardly we are wasting away, yet inwardly we are being renewed day by day. For our light and momentary troubles are achieving for us an eternal glory that far outweighs them all. So we fix our eyes not on what is seen, but on what is unseen. For what is seen is temporary, but what is unseen is eternal (2 Cor. 4:16–18).

It's through suffering, Paul says, that we see what really matters. We're reminded that heaven, not earth, is our final home, that our bodies are corruptible and must decay, that there is an inner life, a spiritual life, that's far more important than the physical one and that we can grow, have hope, and ultimately become better people even though we experience pain.

I hear an echo of Paul's words in the writing of the late Austrian psychiatrist and Holocaust survivor Viktor Frankl, who spoke of man's search for meaning in a world of pain. Frankl wrote,

> What man actually needs is not a tensionless state but rather the striving and struggling for some goal worthy of him. What he needs is not the discharge of tension at any cost, but the call of a potential meaning waiting to be fulfilled by him.[3]

What if God miraculously healed every illness? What if our lives were marvelously free from pain? What if we never experienced stress, anxiety, tension, pain, disease, or frustration? It's very possible that we, like David, like Samson, like so many of the idle rich in our own day, would become obsessed with our bodies, our wealth, and ourselves. In short, we might live our lives without reference to God, without the desire or aim to please him and to become like him. We would be healthy and wealthy and shallow and shortsighted. It is pain, in part, that keeps our eyes on the goal of being authentic citizens of the kingdom of heaven rather than self-satisfied residents of earth.

Grace to Endure

I don't remember all that much about my afternoon of torture. I do recall that it was the worst pain I've ever experienced. Like Paul and countless other sufferers, I cried out for relief. There was none. God did not take the pain away. Yet I survived, and I did so with some measure of dignity. It was not—please believe me—because I have a high pain threshold or because I have some great reserve of inner strength. I managed the day because of God's grace. God helped me bear the pain.

I've heard similar testimony from dozens of pain survivors, like Janet Forsythe, who carried a burden of anger toward her cruel, unloving foster mother for more than a dozen years: "One day I realized that I don't have to carry this anger," she said, "so I let it go." God didn't remove the pain of being unloved, but he helped her cope with it. And consider Laura Johnson, the 26-year-old mother who lost her child to SIDS. Awash in grief, she had abandoned hope of recovery. "Then God called my name," she says calmly. God did not restore the child to life, but he restored hope to Laura's heart.

"I lived on Scripture," said Stephanie Abrams of her ordeal with recovered memories of childhood abuse. Stephanie's relationship with her abusive mother remains broken, but God's Word became a salve for her broken heart.[4]

God didn't remove the pain from any of our lives. My legs still hurt. Laura's son is still gone. Stephanie continues to live with memories of abuse. But each of us discovered the truth of God's Word, given to Paul as he begged for relief: "My grace is sufficient for you." God doesn't always remove pain, but he does provide the strength, courage, grace, and peace to endure it. We believe that suffering is the terminal point of life. When we suffer, we believe, life is over. God knows better. He sees that we can survive and that we will. He gives us grace to endure.

GOD DESTROYS SUFFERING

The great dream of the New World was to create a perfect society. From the Pilgrims, who dreamed of creating a "city set on a hill" to the Oneida Community of New York to the Amana Colony of Iowa, from Harmony, Pennsylvania, to New Harmony, Indiana, utopian idealists have acted out their hopeful vision for the future across the North American landscape. A Mormon editorial in 1842 declared, "Let the division fences be lined with peach and mulberry trees . . . and the houses surrounded with roses and prairie flowers, and their porches covered with grape vine, and we shall soon have formed some idea of how Eden looked."[5] For nearly 400 years we have dreamed of a place where life might be perfect.

We come by that dream honestly. It was planted in our hearts by God himself. For God intends not merely to relieve suffering or to enable us to endure it. He wants nothing less than to destroy it completely.

The Dream

From the beginning God has planned for the end. Since the moment suffering was introduced into the world, he has planned to destroy it. Our clue to this intention comes, oddly enough, along with the curse that God placed on the world after Adam and Eve sinned. Along with a curse upon Eve, who would bear children in pain (see Gen. 3:16), and Adam, who would survive only by painful toil (see Gen. 3:17), and the earth, which would become a wild and dangerous place (see Gen. 3:18), God placed a curse upon the serpent who had tempted Eve to sin:

"You will crawl on your belly and you will eat dust all the days of your life," God said. "And I will put enmity between you and the woman, and between your offspring and hers; he will crush your head, and you will strike his heel" (Gen. 3:14–15).

In addressing the serpent, God was really addressing Satan, who had used the clever animal to do his bidding. The offspring of Eve is Christ. You will wound him, God foretold to Satan, but he will destroy you. The point, simply, is that good will triumph in the end. God will make an end of evil and the suffering that it brings.

The very last book of the Bible makes that even plainer. In John's apocalyptic vision, he saw a new city—a new dwelling place for human beings. He heard a loud voice proclaim,

> Now the dwelling of God is with men, and he will live with them. They will be his people, and God himself will be with them and be their God. He will wipe every tear from their eyes. There will be no more death or mourning or crying or pain, for the old order of things has passed away (Rev. 21:3–4).

It's real. The idyllic, perfect society that dreamers have sought for thousands of years is real. The dream pursued relentlessly by the Curies and Salks of the world, the dream of a day without disease, is real. The dream of a time without war, without famine, without injustice, without pain, without tears, without suffering, without death—it's real. For there will come a time, God has promised, when all evil and the suffering that it brings will be finally destroyed. The question *How long must I endure this?* does have an answer. God will finally relieve all suffering in the end.

Ah, but when will that day come?

The Delay

A recent television advertisement for an over-the-counter pain reliever boasted of its fast action. The competing product, so the ad stated, might take up to 20 minutes to relieve a headache. But this product, gloated the advertisement, would relieve pain in just 10 minutes. "I haven't got time for the pain," declared the pitchwoman, as if 10 minutes of her life were too precious a commodity to be spent in something as banal as restoring health. Yet there's no doubt that the ad connected with its target audience—North American adults. We find pain to be something worse than uncomfortable—it's inconvenient. We want relief from pain, and we want it now! That attitude, so prevalent in our culture, makes it difficult both to endure suffering and to take seriously the idea that God really will abolish suffering at some time. *Why not now?* we wonder. *What's taking so long?*

Some version of that question was asked not more than a few decades after the time of Christ. During the lifetime of the apostle Peter, he warned of scoffers who would challenge the notion that Christ would return to set the world right. Peter predicted that they would belittle the idea that God intends to destroy evil and establish a perfect society. And they would, Peter said, have at least this much ammunition for their argument: for thousands of years the world has continued to exist just as it is today. We have no proof of a time when life was different here on earth and no objective reason to believe that it will ever change. The world turns, people are born, they live, and they die. Life goes on. Why should we believe that will ever change? Adding weight to the argument is the increasing length of time since Jesus walked the earth promising to return. For over 1,900 years we have been waiting for the day described in John's vision. And we're still waiting.

Peter's response to those critics forms one of the most eloquent and most quoted sound bytes in Scripture: "Do not forget this one thing, dear friends: With the Lord a day is like a thousand years, and a thousand years are like a day" (2 Pet. 3:8). God simply doesn't reckon time in the same way we do.

He is on a different schedule, one that doesn't always make sense to us. Peter goes on to explain the reason for God's apparent delay in crushing evil and ridding the world of pain: he is merciful. God simply wants to allow as much time as possible before punishing injustice so that as many people as possible may be brought into his kingdom by faith in Christ. "He is patient with you, not wanting anyone to perish, but everyone to come to repentance" (2 Pet. 3:9).

When will Christ return? When will evil be abolished? When will there be an end to suffering? When will my life be rid of pain? We want the answer now, if not sooner. Yet God knows better than we do that the end of time will mean even greater suffering for much of his beloved creation. Peter describes the scene in graphic detail: "The day of the Lord will come like a thief. The heavens will disappear with a roar; the elements will be destroyed by fire, and the earth and everything in it will be laid bare" (2 Pet. 3:10). That awesome destruction will usher in the new order. Is that to be wished for? Should it be hurried? We could wish for a world without pain, but be careful what you wish for. As Peter reminds us, you just may get it.

KEEP GOING

Mark Vonnegut, son of the novelist Kurt Vonnegut, once made this comment on the purpose of life: "Father, we are here to help each other get through this thing, whatever it is."[6] The advice is biblical. Perseverance is a major theme in the New Testament. Over and over the apostles call us to endure. We're told to "stand firm" (1 Cor. 15:58), "stand fast" (1 Pet. 5:12), and "stand your ground" (Eph. 6:13). Life isn't easy. It takes a certain amount of chutzpah just to survive. We have to keep going.

We could wish life were different, but that's all it would be—a wish. In spite of the fact that Jesus instantly ended the suffering of multitudes of people and that God promises a day when death will die, we live in a world where pain is the daily experience of many, perhaps most, people. We suffer.

Given that suffering is part of the human condition, Guatama Buddha said, "The secret of health for both mind and body is not to mourn for the past, not to worry about the future, or not to anticipate troubles, but to live the present moment wisely and earnestly." Jesus of Nazareth counsels us: "I tell you, do not worry about your life, what you will eat or drink; or about your body, what you will wear. . . But seek first his kingdom and his righteousness" (Matt. 6:25, 33). In this world of woe, we're to trust God and not worry. Is that advice too simple?

God does promise relief from pain, but not this second. God does promise an end to suffering, but perhaps not in your lifetime. God does promise a perfect world, one free from disease and pain and death, but first, says Peter, we may have to suffer "for a little while" (1 Pet. 1:6).

So we endure.

For as Robert Frost put it, "the best way out is always the way through." Or better still, in the words of Winston Churchill, "When you're going through hell, keep going."

QUESTIONS FOR REFLECTION

1. Have you ever wondered why some people are healed from illness—either miraculously or through medical science—and others aren't? What conclusions have you drawn?

2. In your own life, has God more often responded to your plea for relief from suffering by removing the source of suffering or by giving you greater strength to endure?

3. What painful circumstance are you enduring right now? Has that experience had any effect on your relationship with God? If so, what?

4. Do you think about life after death? Do you look forward to it?

8

WHAT'S IN
YOUR HAND?
OUR RESPONSIBILITY
FOR RELIEF

Why doesn't God help those people?

Life's most urgent question is
"What are you doing for others?"
—Martin Luther King Jr.

Sunlight streams through open shutters into the dingy interior of the halfway house. Chantha, a young Cambodian woman, sits on the dusty floor, shooing flies away from her face. "When I was a little girl," she says, "I dreamed of going to school and then finding someone to love, to have a family. That was my dream when I was a little girl. Then I was forced to become a prostitute at age 13."

In a dull monotone, the pathetic creature recounts the details of her miserable young life. Beaten by her stepmother and refused food, Chantha left home to find work. Upon arriving in the city, she was befriended by a woman who promised domestic work in her home. The home was a brothel, and there Chantha was forced to have sex with men. If she refused, she was beaten or shocked with electricity. "There was always someone watching," she says bitterly. "I could not escape." For two years Chantha was forced to serve as a prostitute.

"Finally I convinced the woman to let me go so I could find my father and stepmother," Chantha continues. "But when I found them—" She pauses, looks away. Tears well in her eyes and stream down her cheeks. "When I found them, they despised me and told me to leave."

For three days the helpless teenager lived in the open fields. She had no food, no shelter, no friends. In desperation, she resorted to the only means she knew for generating income. "Hungry and alone, I sat near a garden," she recalls, "and waited for men to come to me." After several customers, she had enough money to buy some food and a one-way bus ticket to the city, hoping at last for a better life.

When Chantha arrived in the city, a man met her at the bus station. He seemed to realize that she was alone, and he offered her a safe place to stay. It seemed like a miracle; she trusted the man and went with him. But he betrayed her trust. The man sold Chantha to another brothel, where she lived as a sex slave, forced to service 15 men each day. If she did not, she was beaten and refused food.

"This is the story of my life," Chantha says, sorrow heavy upon her face. "I am now 24, and I am dying from AIDS. One of my greatest fears is that when I die, no one will come to my burial. When I talk to God, I ask him to give me peace."[1]

Where is God for Chantha, and why has he not given her peace? Where is God for the 100,000 women and girls trapped in Cambodia's sex industry, many of them literally held as slaves? Where is God when girls as young as 7 and 8 are forced into prostitution?[2]

And where is God when 1,400 children in the United States die each year from abuse or neglect?[3] Where is God when 3 million American children go hungry every day?[4] Where is God when some 20 million people die of a disease like AIDS, which infects more than 60 million others, leaving 14 million orphans worldwide?[5] Where is God for the 30 million Africans infected with the AIDS virus, including 3 million children under the age of 15?[6]

Why doesn't God relieve the suffering caused by war or do something about disease, about injustice, about hunger? All these things could be prevented. Why doesn't God do something?

And here's another question: Why don't you?

We Are Responsible

In my home, as in many others, there have been frequent discussions about small matters of injustice. Generally, those began when one of the children would ask some question, usually with a hint of accusation: "Where are the clean towels?" "Who drank all the milk?" "Why are there no clean dishes?" What underlies those questions is a feeling of injustice. *Why should I,* they seem to wonder, *a child in this family, be required to go without fresh towels or milk or clean cereal bowls? How come my parents don't take care of me as they ought to?*

The whole thing became tiresome.

Finally, my wife and I ended the "injustice" in our home by assigning the responsibility for certain chores to each child. Since that day, my son has never asked his mother in an ironic tone, "Where are all the clean towels?" He knows that they're in the dryer, which is where they will stay until he folds them and puts them away. That's his job. And my daughter has never since then asked, "How come there are no clean cereal bowls?" If they're not clean, she knows it's because she has not washed them. She either does so or goes without.

Responsibility is a marvelous thing.

And God has given responsibility to us. It's part of our contract with him, made at the beginning of time.

God Made Us Responsible

When the founders of the United States declared their independence, they drew upon a concept embedded in the very first pages of Scripture: the rights of every human being. "We hold these truths to be self-evident," states the Declaration of Independence, "that all men are created equal, that they are endowed by their creator with certain unalienable rights." Nothing could be truer. Scripture puts it this way:

> So God created man in his own image, in the image of God he created him; male and female he created them (Gen. 1:27).

God made us unique among his creation in that we share his image. We're made to be like God in some sense. That's a privileged condition, and we seem to know that. All over the world, political discussions center on the rights of human beings. We should have liberty. We should be treated with dignity. We should be treated justly. It's this very idea that underlies our question "Why doesn't God do something about suffering?" We know that we should be treated better than we are.

Yet with any right comes responsibility. The very next verse of Scripture declares, "God blessed them and said to them, 'Be fruitful and increase in number; fill the earth and subdue it. Rule over the fish of the sea and the birds of the air and over every living creature that moves on the ground'" (Gen. 1:28). We're given the privilege of sharing God's image, and we're given the corresponding responsibility to exercise his authority over the earth. A theologian would say that we have *dominion* over the earth. A parent would say that we must do our own chores. The practical effect is the same. If my son's room is a mess, it isn't my responsibility to find his socks for him. And if our world is riddled with hunger, poverty, disease, and injustice, it isn't God's job to straighten it up—it's ours. We were given that responsibility at Creation.

It's true that we've been damaged by our sin and the resulting curse that God placed upon the earth. The image of God in us is splintered. Yet it's there. We're thinking beings; we're moral beings. We're able to know God and to become like him through Jesus Christ. And if our ability to control what happens on earth also is compromised, it's not completely ruined. We're given the world to tend, and God expects us to do it. If AIDS is a problem, it's our problem. If hunger is a problem, we're responsible to solve it. If the environment is being destroyed, people refuse to live in peace, and children suffer, these things are so because we've allowed them. There's little use railing at God about problems that are within our power to correct. He's likely to tell us the same thing a mother would tell her son about the need for a freshly pressed shirt—do it yourself.

God Holds Us Accountable

"It ain't those parts of the Bible that I can't understand that bother me," quipped Mark Twain. "It's the parts I *do* understand." There is perhaps no more easily understood yet troublesome portion of Scripture than Jesus' parable of the sheep and goats (see Matt. 28:31–46). In it Jesus tells of the great judgment that will take place at the end of the world. At that time, according to Jesus, God will separate people as a shepherd would separate sheep from goats.

That day, Jesus says, will be like the day when a king returns to his kingdom after a long absence. The king, of course, represents Christ himself. When the king returns, he will report his pleasure at those of his subjects who have shown him mercy by simple acts of kindness such as offering food, shelter, or clothing. And the king will be greatly displeased at those who have ignored him in his time of need.

Naturally, the king's subjects will be confused by this. "Lord," they will ask, "when did we ever see you hungry?" Now comes the climax of Jesus' parable. "I tell you the truth," the king will respond, "whatever you did for one of the least of these brothers of mine, you did for me" (Matt. 25:40). The point is crystal-clear. When we perform simple acts of kindness for others, it is as if we're doing them for Christ. He expects us to treat the homeless, prisoners, AIDS victims, refugees—all who suffer—as if they were Jesus Christ himself.

There's more.

The flip side of that parable is that when we fail to relieve the suffering of others, it's as if we've ignored Christ himself. Jesus goes on to say that those who were able to recognize the "king" in the guise of needy human beings and provide compassion will be rewarded while those who do not will "go away to eternal punishment" (Matt. 25:46)—a steep price to pay for apathy, indifference, selfishness, or any of the other reasons we invent for not showing mercy to those in need.

It's true that the problems of hunger, disease, war, and prejudice are deeply rooted and difficult to solve—perhaps impossible. Jesus himself said that poverty would always exist (see Matt. 26:11). There have always been wars, and there always will be. People abuse one another. Bad things happen. We live in a broken world, after all. What can we do about that? While we can't do everything, we can do something, and God expects that we'll do what we can.

Irish rock star Bono has become well known for his social activism. Interviewed on national television about the pandemic of AIDS in Africa, Bono responded to the notion that the problem is insoluble. The interviewer rightly asserted that international relief is a complex issue. Many foreign governments are corrupt. Many Third World cultures are resistant to change; they persist in harmful, unhealthy practices. It seems a waste of time and energy to throw relief funds at problems that resist solution. *Why should we?* the interviewer wondered. It seems a waste of time. The rock star's answer could have been taken from the pages of Scripture: "God is not going to accept that as an answer," he said.[7] Given the tenor of Christ's parable, it seems Bono may be right.

The apostle James writes,

What good is it, my brothers, if a man claims to have faith but has no deeds? Can such faith save him? Suppose a brother or sister is without clothes and daily food. If one of you says to him, "Go, I wish you well; keep warm and well fed," but does nothing about his physical needs, what good is it? (James 2:14–16).

God expects action. The question has never been "Can we eliminate all suffering in the world?" The real question is "What will I do to help those within my reach?"

Too often the answer is "Nothing." Yet God has made us responsible to relieve the suffering of others, and he will hold us accountable for doing so.

We Are Able

One day Jesus was teaching a large crowd of people. They were eager to hear his words and perhaps witness some miracle. They followed him to a remote place where they stayed with him all day. Toward evening, Jesus' disciples became concerned. The crowd was large, more than 5,000 people, and they had had nothing to eat all day. "Send the people away," the disciples urged Jesus, "so they can go to the surrounding countryside and villages and buy themselves something to eat." It was a reasonable suggestion.

Jesus' response is intriguing. Rather than giving the order to dismiss the crowd, he put the responsibility for solving the problem back on the disciples. "You give them something to eat," he answered.

Impossible! "That would take eight months of a man's wages," they protested. "Are we to go and spend that much on bread and give it to them to eat?" Again, a reasonable response.

And again, Jesus forced the disciples to take responsibility. "How many loaves do you have?" Jesus asked. Finding that they had only five loaves of bread and two dried fish, Jesus blessed the food, multiplied it, and with it fed the entire crowd—with plenty of food left over (Mark 6:36–38).

This may be the best known of all Jesus miracles, and perhaps the most undervalued. The real miracle is not that Jesus had the power to feed 5,000, but that we do. "What do you have?" Jesus seems always to be asking. Why can't you use what's in your hand, apply a little faith, and get something done?

Indeed, why not?

AIDS is a worldwide problem, an epidemic. But have we *no* resources for solving this problem? Sex slavery is a growing problem in Asia, and according to the United States State Department, it's becoming more profitable than drug trafficking.[8] Yet have we no political power? No economic power? No imagination? No heart? Is there truly nothing we can do?

God has given us the responsibility to relieve suffering, and he has given us something more. He has given us the ability to do so. With the power of faith and the fortitude to act, we can make a difference in this world.

Compassion

Before her death in 1997, Princess Diana of Great Britain was one of the most sought-after celebrities in the world. Her innocent beauty, storybook wedding, and tragically unhappy marriage captured the hearts of millions. Many people know that as her personal life deteriorated, the princess threw herself into charity work, spending countless hours listening to the individual stories and problems of the people she visited. We have seen news footage of the elegant princess visiting AIDS wards or sitting beside children whose arms or legs had been mangled by land mines. Yet most people don't know that Diana often took a personal interest in the suffering people she met, sending them personal notes or birthday cards. She understood the power of her public role to direct attention toward social problems, yet she also understood the power of personal contact—including touch—in relieving the pain of suffering people. "Hugs can do a great amount of good," Diana said, "especially for children. . . . I make the trips [to visit AIDS patients] at least three times a week and spend up to four hours at a time with patients, holding their hands and talking with them. Some of them will live and some will die, but they all need to be loved while they are here."[9]

Is there any doubt that this woman changed the world?

The statistics on disease, hunger, child abuse, illiteracy, war, or poverty are overwhelming. We live in a world of great suffering. And Jesus was right—these problems will always exist. But we can relieve the suffering of individuals whom we meet. We cannot eliminate hunger, but we can feed people. We cannot heal all disease, but we can comfort the sick. We cannot eliminate crime, but we can show mercy to criminals and to crime victims. We can offer support, food, shelter, dignity, hope to those we meet. We can create a world in which other people know that in spite of their suffering, they have been loved. There's great power in the simple act of looking a person in the eye, touching his or her hand, and listening. There's greater power in sharing a meal, a garment, or a roof.

What can I do about suffering? we ask.

"What do you have?" Jesus asks in return. Use it, whatever it is, to make the world a better place.

Justice

"We feel and weigh soon enough what we suffer from others," Thomas à Kempis notes in his classic work *The Imitation of Christ,* "but how much others suffer from us, of this we take no heed." We relieve suffering when we show kindness. And we relieve suffering when we do not inflict suffering. When we recognize the effect of our actions on others and begin to live justly, we make the world a better place.

Some of the strongest words in Scripture are reserved for those who either by action or inaction take advantage of the helpless. Jesus was supremely tolerant of human weakness, yet there were things that moved him to anger. Among them were those who lead a child to sin (see Mark 12:40) and those who take advantage of naive or helpless widows (see Luke 20:47). Given those values, we must wonder how Jesus would react to the pornography that we allow to be broadcast on our public airwaves, the shameless marketing of tobacco to children, or the blatant attempts by media producers to make young teenagers slaves to celebrity culture and fashion. And if Jesus were to walk through a nursing home and see the degrading way in which many elderly people are treated while the health-care executives live in luxury, would he not be appalled and angered? The harshest words that Christ directed at anyone would likely be directed at a society like ours, which seems to prey upon children and the elderly: "Such men will be pun-ished most severely" (Mark 12:40).

But what has that to do with *me?* What responsibility could *I* possibly have for the broad-scale problems in this society?

Undoubtedly, most of the people who lived in central Eu-rope during the 1930s and 1940s were decent, law abiding, even God-fearing people. Yet more than eight million of their brethren, Jews, Poles, Gypsies, and others, were exterminated from their midst. Somehow, the majority of the population felt no responsibility for what happened around them. History has judged them differently, as it will undoubtedly judge any socie-ty that tolerates suffering and injustice in its midst. We relieve suffering by acts of kindness, and we relieve suffering by adopt-ing a lifestyle that treats others with dignity. Further, we relieve suffering by working to create a just society, not allowing our-selves to profit—even passively—by the misery of others.

Does the African AIDS epidemic concern us? Is sex traffick-ing in Cambodia any of our business? Do we have anything to do with the wages and working conditions in south China? Do our lives have any impact on the suffering of people whom we've never met? In a world that is often described as a global village, it becomes difficult to argue that our lifestyles and eco-nomic choices have no effect upon others. In a world in which the 100 wealthiest people control fortunes totaling more than $967 billion,[10] nearly twice the annual budget of the United States government for all health and human services,[11] a world in which some five percent of the world's population—a percentage that includes ourselves—consumes some 80 percent of its resources, we might be well advised to consider whether the way in which we live diminishes the suffering of others or adds to it. "No man is an island," wrote John Donne. "Any man's death diminishes me, because I am involved in mankind."[12] We are involved too, and the suffering of any person must have some impact upon our own lives as well.

The name of Eugene Debs has faded from mention in social studies classes. Yet 100 years ago, this labor leader and political activist was one of the driving forces for social justice in the United States. Now long forgotten, his most famous quotation exemplifies the just life that Jesus urged upon us with his simple Golden Rule. Debs said, "Years ago I recognized my kinship with all living things, and I made up my mind that I was not one bit better than the meanest on the earth. I said then and I say now, that while there is a lower class, I am in it; while there is a criminal element, I am of it; while there is a soul in prison, I am not free."[13]

When we see ourselves, our money, our culture, our lifestyle, our choices as tied together with the welfare of all people, we will have less need to ask why people suffer, for at our own hands, they will not.

Evangelism

On August 28, 1963, Martin Luther King Jr. stood on the steps of the Lincoln Memorial in Washington, D.C., and delivered what may be his most powerful speech. To hundreds of thousands of civil rights marchers—and a watching nation—he articulated a vision for a new society with the potent words "I have a dream."

In that famous oration rang the echo of another speech, delivered some centuries earlier on a dusty hillside in Galilee. There Jesus of Nazareth delivered to a vast crowd his declaration of a new society in his Sermon on the Mount (see Matthew 5—7). Jesus envisioned a new world order, one in which the meek would be honored, truth would always be spoken, and neither fists nor words would be used for violence. It would be a world in which all people would treat one another with respect, and even enemies would become friends. Jesus called this new society "the kingdom of heaven."

Is it an impossible dream? Can we create an invisible kingdom on earth whose citizens alleviate suffering by living justly and showing mercy toward one another? Or is evil too deeply ingrained in the human heart? Is it impossible that we could truly change the world, as Christ invited us to do?

The apostle Paul believed in the dream. He knew that while all people are broken by sin, God has the power to change the human heart. In spite of the fact that we're bent toward selfishness, God can fix what ails us. We can be born again. "If anyone is in Christ," Paul wrote, "he is a new creation; the old has gone, the new has come! All this is from God, who reconciled us to himself through Christ and gave us the ministry of reconciliation" (2 Cor. 5:17–18). We can be reconciled both to God and to each other, Paul believed. The notion that we can choose to live according to the kingdom that Jesus described is not a fantasy. God has the power to change the human heart. And we apply that power to others when we introduce them to Jesus Christ.

The greatest program for the relief of suffering in human history is not the New Deal of the 1930s, the Marshall Plan of the 1940s, the Great Society of the 1960s, or even the compassionate conservatism of the 1990s. It's the gospel of Jesus Christ, the good news that the power of sin can be broken in the human heart. We can be reconciled to God. We can be reconciled to one another.

Injustice, poverty, war, hunger, illiteracy, the spread of disease—these evils break out where hatred, prejudice, and ignorance are allowed to exist. And they are all diminished by love and reconciliation. It's no coincidence that thousands of hospitals and schools all over the world bear the names of Christian saints. For where the gospel of Jesus Christ is spread, ministries of compassion flower. God has charged us with the reconciliation of others to themselves and to him. When we fulfill that commission, bringing others to know Jesus Christ, we relieve the suffering of those around us.

A WORLD OF HOPE

Chantha, the Cambodian woman who was forced into the sex trade, was rescued from slavery and supported in her new life by a relief agency known as World Hope International. World Hope is the vision of an American woman named Jo Anne Lyon, the agency's founder and executive director. The vision grew from Jo Anne's lifelong desire to relieve the suffering in others. That desire was born in her, by the Spirit of God, as she grew up as a preacher's kid in rural Kansas during the 1950s. There she saw firsthand the effects of poverty and prejudice on the lives of people. That resolve was strengthened in her as she served as a social worker in Kansas City during the 1970s. There she witnessed the pathetic cycle of domestic abuse and drug dependency that enslaves so many inner-city women. That passion erupted during the 1980s as Jo Anne traveled to refugee camps in Sudan and watched helplessly as children died of starvation before her eyes.

With the support of her husband, Wayne, and encouragement from the director of a global missionary organization, Jo Anne launched World Hope in 1996. Its stated vision is to provide "life, opportunity, dignity, and hope" to those who suffer. The organization's growth has been explosive; it now has independent chapters in the United States, Canada, and Australia and provides community health services, education, micro-enterprise development, and other relief services in more than 30 countries. Tens of thousands of lives have been affected by this agency—the vision of one woman with a passion to relieve the suffering of others.

One of those lives was Chantha's.

As stated earlier, Chantha's greatest fear was that she would die alone, her death unnoticed and her life unremembered. Chantha passed away in February 2003, but she did not die alone. Her pastor was with her as this beautiful young woman was finally freed from her slavery to pain. At her memorial service was one unlikely visitor, a middle-aged American woman with a heart the size of her home state of Kansas, wearing sunglasses to hide her tear-filled eyes. Jo Anne Lyon was there to remember the life of this precious woman who had been unknown and unloved for so long. She was freed from a life of exploitation and cruelty by the compassionate action of a woman from the other side of the world.

Why didn't God do something to help Chantha?

He did.

QUESTIONS FOR REFLECTION

1. What instances of suffering that you have seen in others affect you the most deeply?

2. Do you think Jesus' parable of the sheep and goats should be taken literally? Why or why not?

3. Given the fact that we can't solve all the world's problems, what acts of justice or compassion seem to make the most sense for us to do right now?

4. How many people in your sphere of influence don't know Jesus? What practical things could you do to introduce them to the kingdom of heaven that Jesus talked about?

AFTERWORD
TO THOSE WHO SUFFER

But what thy thorny crown gained, that give me,
A crown of Glory, which does flower always.
—John Donne, "La Corona"

There is no escape from suffering in this life. We would like it, we dream of it, we seek it constantly. Like a modern-day Ponce de Leon, we look for that secret fountain—medicine, cosmetic surgery, wealth—that will ensure a life without suffering. But there is no fountain of youth. While we're alive, we'll feel pain. Suffering is inevitable. We eliminate it where we can, we avoid it whenever possible, but we can't hope for a life on earth that does not include pain.

What we need, then, is to cope with suffering. We must learn to tolerate it when necessary, to admit its presence without desiring it, to see it as a regrettable part of life but not the end of life.

How do we do that?

I believe it helps us to know that we're united with the Lord in our suffering. Jesus died. That must be the cornerstone of what we believe about our own suffering. For if Jesus died, then we know that we must die too. And if he chose to suffer—yet was made perfect by it—then there must be some value in our suffering as well. "I want to know Christ," Paul said, and part of that knowing meant sharing in Christ's suffering and death (see Phil. 3:10–11). Being united with Christ in his suffering lets us know that we're not alone. Everyone suffers; even God suffered. So our suffering brings us into fellowship with all human beings and even with God himself. We must remember that only plastic people live perfect lives. All real people suffer.

Yet if we suffer, we also seek relief. And relief from pain is best found in community, not in isolation. I recall a television interview of a registered nurse in which the host asked her, "Are you a lifesaving nurse or a hand-holding nurse?"

"I'm a hand-holder," the woman replied. "I'm not the first to jump into a trauma situation, but I come along and hold the patient's hand. I let the patient know that he or she is not alone."

Bravo for that woman! The world needs more hand-holding nurses. And more of us who suffer need to be willing to open our hands. We prefer to deal with pain in isolation because we're embarrassed about being human, but it's our contact with others that truly relieves suffering. Most pain, after all, cannot be relieved by medicine, surgery, or courts of law. Most of what we suffer we must endure. And the presence of others, perhaps more than anything else, helps us to endure, to stay sane, even though we're in pain. We need each other.

Ultimately, though, we endure suffering by choosing to endure. When we suffer, our temptation is to believe in the pain and doubt the Lord. We may come to see the world as evil and our lives as meaningless. When that happens, we must make the choice to believe. We must make the choice to trust God and to redeem our experience. Viktor Frankl writes,

> We who lived in concentration camps can remember the men who walked through the huts comforting others, giving away their last piece of bread. They may have been few in number, but they offer sufficient proof that everything can be taken from a man but one thing: the last of the human freedoms—to choose one's attitude in any given set of circumstances, to choose one's own way.[1]

We have that power to choose. We can choose to be authentic human beings in spite of our pain. We can choose to be Christ followers in spite of the fact—and perhaps *because* of the fact—that we suffer. Pain is a factor in our lives, but it's not the governing factor. We've been created in the image of God, and we're able to make choices. We can choose to redeem our suffering by allowing it to shape our lives in a positive way, by allowing it to bring within us something beautiful, something glorious—like faith and love and hope.

Words, finally, are an ineffective means of coping with suffering. That's why, I believe, Jesus left us with symbols. For on the night he was betrayed, Jesus took bread and broke it. "This is my body," he said. "It is broken for you. Take it and eat it."

In the same way, after supper, he took a cup and said, "This cup is the new deal between you and God. The contract is signed with my blood. Drink it, all of you."

Even though Jesus was the Son of God, he was made perfect by what he suffered. Only then was he able to be ultimately effective in bringing us close to God. That means that our lives and his life and God are all tied up in the fact of suffering. It's when we suffer that we become like Christ in life, like him in death, and like him in his glory.

So whenever we gather together, we come back to this table, the place where God came closest to man. Here we remember the fact that Jesus chose to die, we make sense of our own suffering, and we hope for the day when there will be no pain. For whenever we eat this bread and drink this cup, we proclaim the Lord's death until he comes.

Notes

Introduction

1. Diana Lynne, "Petitions Seek to Defend God: Citizens Swamp Effort to Protect Pledge, Motto after Court Ruling," WorldNetDaily, March 5, 2003, <http://www.worldnetdaily.com/news/article.asp/ARTICLE_ID=31368>.

2. Luke 23:8–9. Also, the Book of Job reveals that God usually says nothing to defend himself against criticism.

3. "Nazi Human Experimentation," *Wikipedia: The Free Encyclopedia*, April 13, 2004, <http://en.wikipedia.org/wiki/Nazi_human_experimentation>.

4. This subject is treated in more detail in chapter 2 of this book.

5. Nathaniel Hawthorne, "Young Goodman Brown," *The Signet Classic Book of American Short Stories*, ed. Burton Raffel (New York: Penguin Books, 1985), 57.

Chapter 1

1. Gregory J. Wilcox, "Adult Film Industry Shuts Down," *Salt Lake Tribune*, April 16, 2004, <http://www.sltrib.com/2004/Apr/04162004/nation_w/157707.asp>.

2. "It's all about you!" is, in fact, the motto of Day-Timers Inc., a publisher of time management resources.

3. Helene Lesel, "Tenants, avoid debt through a lifestyle review," *Charlotte Observer,* April 17, 2004, <http://www.charlotte.com/mld/charlotte/living/home/8453119.htm?1c>.

4. AP Wire, April 9, 2004, <http://www.kait8.com/Global/story.asp/S=1775360&nav=0jshMBup>.

5. Aetna IntelliHealth, "Pain," April 17, 2004, <http://www.kait8.com/Global/story.asp/S=1775360&nav=0jshMBup>.

6. C. S. Lewis, *The Problem of Pain.*

7. Geoff Watts, "Living with Pain," BBC Radio 4 Web site, September 17, 2002, <http://www.bbc.co.uk/radio4/science/livingwithpain.shtml>.

8. Elisabeth Kübler Ross, "Kubler Ross Quotes," April 17, 2004, <http://www.elisabethkublerross.com/pages/Quotes.html>.

Chapter 2

1. Thomas Aquinas, *Summa Contra Gentiles*, cited in Margaret Pepper, *The Harper Religious and Inspirational Quotation Companion* (New York: Harper & Row Publishers, 1989), 215.

2. The creation of Adam and Eve and hints about what life was like in the Garden of Eden are found in Gen. 2:8–25.

3. *The Taming of the Shrew*, Act 1, Scene 1.

4. The curse is spelled out in Gen. 3:14–24.

5. See Gen. 1:27. Many theologians believe that the *imago dei*, the image of God, refers to our free moral agency—the fact that we're given the ability to make meaningful choices.

Chapter 3

1. The birth of Isaac is foretold in Gen. 18:9–15.

2. See Gen. 6:5–6. The prohibition against murder predates the Ten Commandments, which are given in Exod. 20.

Chapter 4

1. Bread for the World Institute, "Hunger Basics: Frequently Asked Questions," July 31, 2004, <http://www.bread.org/hungerbasics/domestic.html>.

2. Forbes.com Inc., "World's Richest People," February 6, 2004, <http://www.forbes.com/maserati/billionaires2004/bill04land.html>.

3. Bread for the World Institute, "Hunger Basics: Domestic Hunger & Poverty Facts," July 13, 2004, <http://www.bread.org/hungerbasics/faq.html>.

4. Centers for Disease Control, "Child Maltreatment Fact Sheet," July 26, 2004, <http://nccanch.acf.hhs.gov/pubs/factsheets/fatality.cfm>.

5. The White House Internet site, "Fact Sheet: The President's Emergency Plan for AIDS Relief," January 2003, <http://www.whitehouse.gov/news/releases/2003/01/20030129-1.html>.

6. Richard Willing, "States target unsolved murders: Arrest of alleged serial killer prompts new look into dozens of cases," detnews.com, June 5, 2003, <http://www.detnews.com/2003/nation/0306/05/a15d-183722.htm.>

7. Robert McAfee Brown, "Introduction," in Elie Wiesel, *The Trial of God*, trans. Marion Wiesel (New York: Schocken Books, 1979, 1995), vii.

Chapter 5

1. American Society of Plastic Surgeons, "2003 Gender Distribu-

tion: Cosmetic Procedures," August 3, 2004, <http://www.plasticsurgery.org/public_education/loader.cfm?url=/commonspot/security/getfile.cfm&PageID=13620>.

2. Ibid.

3. See Isa. 53:2. This prophecy about the Christ is usually interpreted to mean that Jesus was not a physically attractive man.

4. John Donne, "Nativitie," *Holy Sonnets.*

5. "Halle swipes at plastic copycat look," The Advertiser.com, August 4, 2004, <http://www.theadvertiser.news.com.au/common/story_page/0,5936,10338363%255E912,00.html>.

6. Elbert Hubbard, *Epigrams.* (QuotationLibrary.com, 27 November 2004)

Chapter 6

1. The award was created first for the Navy (December 1861) and later for the Army (July 1862). The words "gallantry in action" appear in both S. No. 82, which created the award for the Navy, and S. J. R. No. 82, which created the award for the Army.

2. Michael Taylor, "Tracking Down False Heroes: Medal of Honor recipients go after imposters," SFGate.com, May 31, 1999, <http://sfgate.com/cgi-bin/article.cgi?file=/chronicle/archive/1999/05/31/MN106963.DTL&type=printable>.

3. Ibid.

4. Terry and Jim Willard, "Step 9: Immigration Records," Ancestry.com, May-June 2000, <http://www.ancestry.com/learn/library/article.aspx/article=2043>.

5. Information from the United States Department of Defense and Veterans Administration, cited in "America's Wars: U. S. Casualties and Veterans," Information Please, September 4 2004, <http://www.infoplease.com/ipa/A0004615.html>.

Includes data from the American Revolution through the 1991 Gulf War.

6. Elisabeth Kübler-Ross, <http://www.elisabethkublerross.com/pages/Quotes.html, April 17, 2004>.

7. Quoted in Margaret Pepper, *The Harper Religious and Inspirational Quotation Companion* (New York: Harper and Row Publishers, 1989), 407.

8. Elbert Hubbard, *The Note Book.* (QuotationLibrary.com, 27 November 2004)

9. United States Army Center of Military History, "Medal of Honor Recipients: Somalia," <http://www.army.mil/cmh-pg/mohsom.htm>, June 5, 2004.

Chapter 7

1. Pacific College of Oriental Medicine, "Acupuncture as Effective as Drug Therapy for Migraines & Headaches," April 24, 2004, <http://www.pacificcollege.edu/news/press_releases/2004/TCM_for_migraines.htm>.

2. Medstar.com, "Doctors save baby's life with surgery before birth," News14.com, August 2, 2004, <http://rdu.news14.com/content/health_and_fitness/ArID=52404&SecID=376>.

3. Viktor E. Frankl, *Man's Search for Meaning* (New York: Washington Square Press, 1963), 166.

4. The stories of Janet, Laura, and Stephanie are told in greater detail in *When Life Doesn't Turn Out the Way You Expect,* by Jerry Brecheisen and Lawrence W. Wilson (Kansas City: Beacon Hill Press of Kansas City, 2004), chapters 1, 3-4.

5. Peter N. Herndon, "Utopian Communities, 1800-1890," Yale New Haven Teacher's Institute, 2004, <http://www.yale.edu/ynhti/curriculum/units/1989/1/89.01.04.x.html>.

6. Kurt Vonnegut, "Cold Turkey," *In These Times*, May 10, 2004, <http://www.inthesetimes.com/site/main/article/cold_turkey/>.

Chapter 8

1. World Hope International, "Chantha's Story" online video, September 16, 2004, <http://www.frankherrmann.com/frankherrmann/whi/cambodia_menu.html>.

2. Ibid.

3. United States Department of Health and Human Services, Administration for Children and Families, "Child Abuse and Neglect Fatality Statistics," May 2004, <http://nccanch.acf.hhs.gov/pubs/factsheets/fatality.pdf>.

4. Bread for the World Institute, "Hunger Basics: Domestic Hunger and Poverty Facts," April 8, 2004, http://www.bread.org/hungerbasics/domestic.html.

5. The White House, "Fact Sheet: The President's Emergency Plan for AIDS Relief," January 29, 2004, <http://www.whitehouse.gov/news/releases/2003/01/20030129-1.html>.

6. Ibid.

7. Fox News Channel, "Bono: Not Facing AIDS Crisis 'Foolhardy,'" September 2, 2004, <http://www.foxnews.com/story/0,2933,131198,00.html>.

8. World Hope International, "Chantha's Story."

9. "In Her Own Words," Diana: The Work Continues, July 16, 2004, <http://www.theworkcontinues.org/aboutus/inherownwords.asp>.

10. Forbes.com, "Special Report: The World's Richest People," February 26, 2004, <http://www.forbes.com/maserati/billionaires2004/bill04land.html>.

11. Government Printing Office, "Budget of the United States Government: Browse Fiscal Year 2005," *GPO Access,* July 30, 2004, <http://www.gpoaccess.gov/usbudget/fy05/browse.html>.

12. John Donne, "Devotions upon Emergent Occasions." *The Complete Poetry and Prose of John Donne,* Charles M. Coffin, ed., (New York: The Modern Library, 1994), 441.

13. United States Department of Labor, Office of the Assistant Secretary for Administration and Management, "Labor Hall of Fame Honoree: 1990 Honoree Eugene V. Debs, 1855—1926," September 16, 2004, <http://library.dol.gov/oasam/programs/laborhall/evd.htm>.

Afterword

1. Frankl, *Man's Search for Meaning,* 104.